T0028594

SACRED SEASONS

SACRED SEASONS

*Nature-Inspired Rituals,
Wisdom, and Self-Care for
Every Day of the Year*

KIRSTY
GALLAGHER

RUNNING PRESS
PHILADELPHIA

Copyright © 2023 by Kirsty Gallagher
Cover copyright © 2023 by Hachette Book Group, Inc.

Hachette Book Group supports the right to free expression and the value of copyright. The purpose of copyright is to encourage writers and artists to produce the creative works that enrich our culture.

The scanning, uploading, and distribution of this book without permission is a theft of the author's intellectual property. If you would like permission to use material from the book (other than for review purposes), please contact permissions@hbgusa.com. Thank you for your support of the author's rights.

Running Press
Hachette Book Group
1290 Avenue of the Americas, New York, NY 10104
www.runningpress.com
@Running_Press

Printed in the United States of America

Originally published in 2023 by Yellow Kite in the United Kingdom.
First U.S. Edition: June 2023

Published by Running Press, an imprint of Perseus Books, LLC, a subsidiary of Hachette Book Group, Inc. The Running Press name and logo are trademarks of the Hachette Book Group.

Running Press books may be purchased in bulk for business, educational, or promotional use. For more information, please contact your local bookseller or the Hachette Book Group Special Markets Department at Special.Markets@hbgusa.com.

The publisher is not responsible for websites (or their content) that are not owned by the publisher.

Print book cover design by Frances J. Soo Ping Chow.
Print book cover art: Getty Images

Library of Congress Cataloging-in-Publication Data has been applied for.

ISBNs: 978-0-7624-8456-0 (hardcover), 978-0-7624-8457-7 (ebook)

LSC-C

Printing 1, 2023

To Nature, for being my greatest teacher
and always showing me the way.

v

CONTENTS

INTRODUCTION   1

Part I: The Background

CHAPTER 1: How to Work with the Seasons   9

CHAPTER 2: Getting to Know the Seasons
and the Wheel of the Year   15

CHAPTER 3: The Moon Through the Seasons   33

CHAPTER 4: Connecting Back to Nature   39

CHAPTER 5: The Wisdom of Nature   47

      Your Nature Wisdom   54

Part II: The Practices

CHAPTER 6: Start-of-spring Season—the Sacred
Season for Awakening *21 March–19 April*   63

CHAPTER 7: Mid-spring Season—the Sacred
Season for Living in Expectation *20 April–20 May*   77

CHAPTER 8: End-of-spring Season—the Sacred
Season for Change and Growth *21 May–20 June*   91

CHAPTER 9: Start-of-summer Season—the Sacred Season for Opportunities *21 June–22 July*   103

CHAPTER 10: Mid-summer Season—the Sacred Season for Abundance *23 July–22 August*   117

CHAPTER 11: End-of-summer Season—the Sacred Season for Getting Back on Track
23 August–21 September   131

CHAPTER 12: Start-of-autumn Season—the Sacred Season for Gratitude *22 September–22 October*   143

CHAPTER 13: Mid-autumn Season—the Sacred Season for Alchemy and Transformation
23 October–21 November   157

CHAPTER 14: End-of-autumn Season
—the Sacred Season for Journeying Inwards
22 November–20 December   171

CHAPTER 15: Start-of-winter Season—the Sacred Season for Looking to the Light
21 December–19 January   183

CHAPTER 16: Mid-winter Season—the Sacred Season for Envisioning and Emerging
20 January–18 February   197

CHAPTER 17: End-of-winter Season—the Sacred Season for Endings and Beginnings *19 February–20 March*   211

CONCLUSION   221

ACKNOWLEDGMENTS   223

ABOUT THE AUTHOR   225

SACRED SEASONS

INTRODUCTION

Welcome to *Sacred Seasons*, a book that has been stirring within me for a long time, just waiting for the right time to be brought into the world.

That time is now.

As difficult and challenging as the last few years have been, during, and since the COVID-19 pandemic, I feel that one of the greatest gifts these years gave us was the opportunity to slow down. Previously, we spent so much of our time indoors, running from home to car to public transportation to office to gym or bar or restaurant and back again. But suddenly, in lockdown, our only option for taking a break from our newly set-up home offices was the hour-long window we got to go outside for a walk.

And I believe this is where magic happened.

 We began to take in the natural world around us. Following the same walking route every day gave us a chance to witness Nature moving through her seasons. The tree that one day was in full bloom, over the months began to shed its leaves, going through a death-and-rebirth process, back to full bloom. We saw snowdrops and bluebells and daffodils. We heard birdsong.

We connected back to Nature, her seasons and her cycles. And I believe that something shifted and stirred within us.

Nature healed us. She held us, she taught us. Just as she always had and always will. But now, perhaps for the first time, many of us were listening.

And it wasn't only the earth that grabbed our attention; it was also the skies. More people than ever before noticed the moon in the sky and developed an interest in astrology and spirituality. I'm often asked why I think that is, and I always give the same answer: we were all looking for connection.

In a time that felt so disconnecting, confusing, and isolating, it was a comfort to know that Nature was a constant all around us and that, wherever we were, all of us were looking at the same moon in the same sky.

And then there was the search for answers. In a world that suddenly no longer made any sense, we did what our ancestors did for thousands of years: we sought answers and solace in Nature and the skies. I've spoken to so many people who say that in the months and years of the pandemic, they felt a deep connection to Nature but weren't sure what it meant or how to deepen it and keep it alive.

I hope that these pages will hold the answers.

About This Book

This book is designed to be a companion, a guide, a mentor, a friend. My hope is that you will keep it by your side as you journey through life, referring to and working with it often.

One of the original meanings of the word "sacred" is "entitled to reverence and respect." My aim with this book is that you will make each season sacred—not only in Nature, but in your life, too. As with Nature, there will be times in your life when you're in full bloom and growing, and others when you feel like you are in a void and everything is falling away. The seasons of Nature mirror the ever-changing seasons of our lives, teaching us how to adapt, flow with, and honor them, treating each turning point, change, and transition with reverence and respect.

This book will take you on a year-long journey to help get you back into alignment with Nature, establishing a rhythm and flow of natural cycles that keep everything moving. A journey which keeps you in tune and connected, not only with Nature but with your own true nature and, in turn, with the seasons of your life, and yourself.

PART I: THE BACKGROUND

Part I will provide you with the all the information you need to understand the why, what, and how of sacred seasons and connecting back to Nature. I will explain, among other things, the Wheel of the Year (an annual cycle marking the seasonal shifts in Nature), astrological seasons, Nature's seasons, what we can learn from Nature and why and how we should live once more in alignment with her.

PART II: THE PRACTICES

Part II is split into twelve chapters, taking you through every season from the beginning and middle to the end, on a year-long journey alongside Nature, her seasons and cycles.

We open with the start-of-spring season, which includes Aries season and the spring equinox, as this is the beginning of the astrological year and the perfect time to start to live in a new way. But, in truth, this book can be started in any season, at any time.

Each chapter includes a sacred pause—a moment, as the season turns, to reflect on where you are and to prepare for where you want to go in the next season. All too often, we rush through the year—and life—never stopping, never checking in, and in doing so, we lose, scatter and abandon ourselves along the way. We get disconnected—not only from Nature and her rhythms, but also from ourselves. Pausing at the start of each season and reflecting on its energies will help you to align with Nature, the earth, and yourself.

Where a Wheel-of-the-Year celebration falls in that season, I have shared all you need to know about marking this transitional turning point, providing practices and rituals to honor each one. Taking time at each turning point of the Wheel of the Year recognizes not only this transitional time in Nature, but also in your own life, evolution, and journey. I see these as markers in your life— opportunities to pause, take stock, and connect back to yourself and the journey of your soul, helping you to form conscious realizations and make changes in accordance with the seasons to keep you and your life in a beautiful state of flow.

Each chapter also gives you information on the relevant zodiac season and ways to connect and work with its energies, as well as insight into the new and full moon that will fall in that season and ways to harness the lunar energies through mini moon rituals.

I also share altar and ritual ideas to help you develop a daily devotional practice for each season and ways to connect with Nature as you move through the seasons.

How to Use This Book

You may choose to dive in fully—take the sacred pause at the beginning of each season, work with the zodiac energies and each of the eight Wheel-of-the-Year celebrations, create an altar, form a daily ritual practice, and celebrate the new and full moon during each season. But for some of you, this may feel like too much, in which case you may simply honor the sacred pause and Wheel-of-the-Year celebrations, dipping in and out of the rest when you need extra support or guidance from the natural world around you. To help with this, I have provided "Sacred Season Made Simple" entries at the end of each chapter, giving you a brief overview of how best to attune to the energies of the season in question. I have also included moments of reflection, and I'd love you to take the opportunity to do just that—reflect on what you want and will commit to doing in the relevant season.

This book is not designed to be something you read, nod along to, and then put to one side. I want you to use it to help create real, tangible, lasting change in your life; and for this to happen, you need to take action, do the inner work, and hold yourself accountable.

Knowledge only becomes wisdom when it's embodied, and that means taking what you are learning through Nature, her season and cycles and celebrations, and applying it to your own life. This will give you a lived experience of what it means to grow, let go, and move through transitions and cycles of your own.

As you work your way through the chapters, please find your

own rhythm and approaches to connecting with Nature. What is important is that you show up for yourself and mark these turning points—Nature's, the zodiac's, and your own—as this is when you will feel the biggest difference in your way of life, and how you will forge a deeper connection to the wisdom of Nature, and therefore yourself.

So pull this book out at the beginning of each season, or any time you feel a little lost, and allow Nature to gift you the answers and wisdom to connect you back to yourself.

PART I

The Background

CHAPTER 1

How to Work with the Seasons

To help you get the most out of *Sacred Seasons*, this chapter contains some important information and a few things you may want to consider before moving on to Part II.

Sacred Seasons Journal

I would suggest getting a special journal for your sacred seasons journey. This way you can journal on the prompts given to you in the sacred pause at the beginning of each season and in the Wheel-of-the-Year celebrations. You can also journal on the new and full moons, your reflection moment, what you are observing and connecting to in Nature, and anything else that is calling your attention as you move through the season.

Journaling is one of the best ways to get to know yourself and your inner world. Putting what you are thinking and how you are feeling on paper helps you to recognize patterns, themes, and progress and, in turn, to process them. It's a powerful tool for self-awareness, self-expression, and self-understanding.

Creating Rituals

We have many routines in life but very few rituals.

The main difference between a routine and a ritual is the attitude behind the action. While a routine is usually more mundane and done out of duty or the need to get something done, a ritual makes something sacred. It gives it a deeper meaning and offers a pause to truly connect with what you are doing.

Daily rituals have always been incredibly important to me—a time that I dedicate to myself, my growth, and my journey.

A ritual can be as simple as lighting a candle to welcome yourself into the day, placing your hands over your heart and checking in with yourself, repeating affirmations (see p. 13), connecting to your intentions (see p. 13), meditating (perhaps with a crystal, if you use them in your practice), and/or journaling.

In each chapter, I offer suggestions to help you create a daily ritual for yourself. Feel free to try these to begin with, but, over time, learn to trust in yourself and what *you* most need, as you flow through the seasons and cycles of the year. The most important thing is not necessarily *what* you do, but that you show up every day for yourself and do it. It's in these moments of showing up every day that you will notice the biggest changes and transformations over time.

The Wheel-of-the-Year celebrations mark the turning point of the season, so I will give you rituals for each of these, too, to help you reflect on where you are, so that you can transition into a new season.

Sacred Seasons Altar

An altar is a sacred space that you use for your daily rituals. It can be as simple as a shelf or a small space in the corner of a room, and it's where you go to perform your rituals and connect with yourself. My altar is an integral part of my daily practice, and I hope that it will be the same for you.

I will give you altar ideas in each season, so that you can connect more deeply to your daily rituals and the seasons' energies. You may choose to change your altar at the start of each major sacred season (spring, summer, autumn, winter) or once a month, as the seasons flow.

You can decorate your altar with a colored cloth and add flowers, images, or things that you collect from Nature that signify the current season. You can also add anything that represents what you want to embody, manifest, and connect to during that season.

Before you "build" your altar, get clear on what you want to create and manifest in your life, so that it holds the energy of whatever you want to devote your attention to over the coming season.

There is always a candle on my altar that I light daily as a means of connection to myself and the day ahead. I also always have a crystal grid there that holds the energy of my intentions for the lunar cycle or season ahead. (Simply put, a crystal grid is when you arrange crystals with an intention for a desired result; for more on how to work with crystals and grids, check out my book *Crystals for*

Self-Care.) You can also have just one crystal on your altar that you connect to daily.

If you are using intentions and affirmations (see p. 13), you can write them out and place them on your altar, under your candle (or crystal, if you are using one). If you keep your intentions under your candle, imagine sending more energy to them each time you light your flame; if you keep them under a crystal, it will continue to amplify your intentions, drawing to you what you need, even when you are not there.

I will give you suggestions for candles, crystals, affirmations, and much more for each season, but again, please feel free to use your intuition and add other things that feel right or are meaningful to you.

Crystal Magic

For each season I will give you suggestions for crystals to work with that resonate with the energy of the season and/or zodiac sign in question. I have tried to use the more common and easily accessible ones and, occasionally, the same ones in different seasons, so you can get the most out of your collection.

You may choose to set your intentions for each season on these crystals and carry them around with you, keep them on your altar or as part of a seasonal crystal grid. You can also meditate with them every day to connect with their energy and your intention.

For an easy grid for your altar, take the crystal you are working with for that season, set your intention for the season on it and then surround it with four clear-quartz points. The grid will then hold and amplify the energy of your intentions for the season.

Intention Setting

Setting intentions is incredibly important as they give our lives direction, meaning, and something to aim for and grow toward. They become a guiding force that helps us to align our thoughts, actions, words, choices, and energy in the pursuit of what we want.

You may choose to set intentions at the start of each season, at each new moon, or even both. I very often set smaller intentions with each new moon and then, at the start of each season, I'll set bigger ones that I want to work with over the full three months.

Writing down your intentions gives them extra weight, as does saying them out loud. Like spells, our words have such incredible power, so repeat your intentions aloud to yourself when you set them, and once a day as part of your ritual, if you can.

Affirmations

Affirmations are positive statements that you repeat to yourself over and over to reprogram your thoughts, helping you to overcome doubts and fears, and improve your self-belief. They can be a powerful tool for helping you to embody the energy of each season and use it to the full.

Affirmations need to be in the present tense, contain only positive words (so rather than saying, "I release doubt," you'd say, "I trust in myself") and be specific and clear.

I will give you examples of affirmations for each season, but feel free to get creative and use your own, especially if there is something you want to work on or manifest in that season.

Gathering with Others

You can do everything in this book alone and take so much from it that way, but I feel that now, more than ever, we need to come together in community. And so, just as our ancestors did, you may choose to gather with others and share these transitional points in Nature and our lives.

Celebrate the turning points of the Wheel of the Year with friends and family, teach your little ones to embrace a natural way of living, create a WhatsApp group with your friends to share your sacred pauses and what you are learning.

Being part of a community gives us a deeper sense of belonging and further reminds us that we are all connected and part of this beautiful world we live in.

CHAPTER 2

Getting to Know the Seasons and the Wheel of the Year

In this book, I will weave the wisdom of Nature with the Wheel-of-the-Year celebrations and astrological seasons, taking you on a year-long journey to come back into alignment—not only with Nature, seasons and cycles, but also with yourself.

Just as we, at our very essence, are connected to Nature, her seasons and cycles are intrinsically connected to the Wheel of the Year and the astrological seasons.

As the earth moves around the sun (at a slight slant, which is what gives us seasons), the sun, from our vantage point on earth, appears to move through the sky, along what is known as the ecliptic. The constellations of the zodiac run just above the ecliptic, meaning that, throughout the year, the sun moves through each sign of the zodiac. It is the date the sun goes into the cardinal signs of the zodiac (Aries, Cancer, Libra, and Capricorn) that marks the solstices and equinoxes, and this, in turn, marks the beginning of Nature's seasons.

Throughout this book, I will refer to the astronomical seasons, which use the dates of the solstices and equinoxes to mark the beginning and end of each of Nature's seasons. In astronomy, for example, spring begins on the day of the spring equinox, when the sun moves into Aries (approximately 21 March) and runs until the summer solstice, when the sun moves into Cancer (approximately 21 June). According to the meteorological seasons, however, spring runs from 1 March to 31 May.

The date the sun moves into the different zodiac signs (and therefore the dates of the solstices and equinoxes) can shift by a day or so either side, year on year. This is because we count a calendar year as 365 days (or 366 in a leap year), but the earth takes 365.24 days (or 365 days, 5 hours, and 48 minutes) to orbit the sun.

Leap years were created to compensate for that extra quarter of a day/six hours a year to better match our calendar year with the solar year, and keep the seasons, solstices, and equinoxes in line with the calendar. But those leap years every four years mean the day and time the sun shifts into the different signs can move by a day or so.

It is also worth briefly mentioning here the difference and relationship between astrology and astronomy: astronomy is the scientific study of the stars, planets, and the galaxies; astrology is the study of how the movement of these planets and stars influences human life. Astronomy and astrology were studied together until the seventeenth century when they were separated into two disciplines.

Note: the seasons in the northern hemisphere are the opposite of those in the southern hemisphere. So to my southern-hemisphere friends: please adapt the seasons where necessary. Now that we know a little more about how Nature's seasons connect with the Wheel of the Year and the astrological seasons, let's take a look at this in slightly more depth.

The Wheel of the Year

The Wheel of the Year consists of eight annual celebrations that mark the turning of the seasons. These moments of pause between seasonal shifts keep us connected to Nature and give us an anchor through which we may pause, reflect, give thanks, and make conscious changes in our own lives before moving into a new season.

There are four fixed quarter points in the year: two solstices and two equinoxes. These represent the beginning of a new season and are celebrated on the day when the sun moves into the cardinal zodiac signs. The four quarter points are then crossed again by the four cross-quarter festivals; these fall at the peak of each season at the exact astrological midpoint between the solstices and the equinoxes (see p. 20).

Here is a list of the eight celebrations:

Spring equinox (Ostara):
- ◆ 20–23 March (northern hemisphere)
- ◆ 20-23 September (southern hemisphere)
- ◆ Sun 0° Aries

The Wheel of the Year

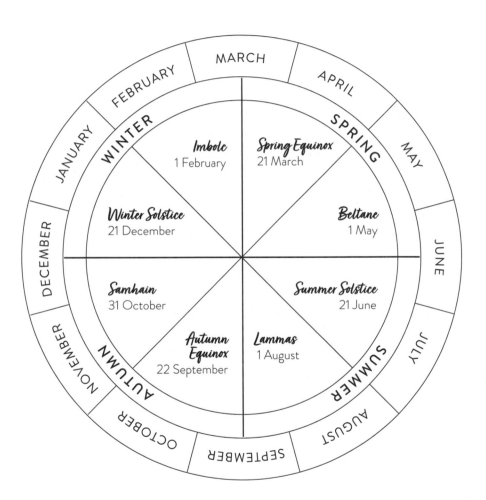

Beltane:
- 1 May (northern hemisphere)
- 31 October (southern hemisphere)
- Sun 15° Taurus

Summer solstice (Litha):
- 20–23 June (northern hemisphere)
- 20–23 December (southern hemisphere)
- Sun 0° Cancer

Lammas (Lughnasadh):
- 1 August (northern hemisphere)
- 1–2 February (southern hemisphere)
- Sun 15° Leo

Autumn equinox (Mabon):
- 20–23 September (northern hemisphere)
- 20–23 March (southern hemisphere)
- Sun 0° Libra

Samhain (Halloween):
- 31 October (northern hemisphere)
- 1 May (southern hemisphere)
- Sun 15° Scorpio

Winter solstice (Yule):
- 20–23 December (northern hemisphere)
- 20–23 June (southern hemisphere)
- Sun 0° Capricorn

Imbolc:

- ◆ 1–2 February (northern hemisphere)
- ◆ 1–2 August (southern hemisphere)
- ◆ Sun 15° Aquarius

THE SOLSTICES

The word solstice means stopping or standing still, from the Latin words *solstitum*—*sol* (sun) and *stitum* (to stop).

The summer solstice occurs in June when the sun is at its farthest north and highest point in the sky, bringing us the longest day of the year and marking the start of summer. The winter solstice occurs in December when the sun is at its farthest south and lowest point in the sky bringing us the shortest day of the year and marking the start of winter. These days—at the midpoint and end of the traditional year—are the ideal time to be still and check in with where you are.

THE EQUINOXES

The word equinox means equal, from the Latin words *aequi* (equal) and *nox* (night).

Equinoxes occur when the sun crosses and appears directly above the equator, making day and night of equal length. The spring equinox in March marks the start of spring and the autumn equinox in September marks the start of autumn; as such, they offer a moment of pause for you to catch up with yourself once again and stand poised in the present, before tipping over the edge into a new season.

THE CROSS-QUARTER FESTIVALS

The cross-quarter festivals are also known as the four great fire festivals and occur when the energy of each season has reached its peak and the signs of the next season are beginning to show.

They were traditionally celebrated when the sun reached the halfway point (15°) of the fixed zodiac signs. As this date changes slightly year on year, dates have been agreed upon when the crossquarter festivals are commonly celebrated, approximately midway through the fixed zodiac sign seasons. However, some people still choose to celebrate on the exact dates of the sun's arrival at 15°, on the nearest full moon to the midpoint or simply when the energy feels right, and Nature and the weather are reflecting the seasonal shift.

The cross-quarter festival celebrations can go on for some time, often beginning at sunrise of one day and closing at sunset the next. The elements are strongly associated with the quarter points with Beltane falling in Taurus (an earth sign), Lammas falling in Leo (a fire sign), Samhain falling in Scorpio (a water sign) and Imbolc falling in Aquarius (an air sign).

HISTORY OF THE WHEEL OF THE YEAR

Celebrations of the Wheel of the Year can be traced all the way back to the neolithic era in 10,200 BC, when they were understood to have marked the solstices and equinoxes. This period saw the transition from nomadic bands of hunter gatherers to people starting to live together in communities and farming the land.

Later, the Anglo Saxons, who were mainly pagans, were also believed to have held celebrations and rituals on the solstices and equinoxes, observing the turning points in Nature and praying to their gods and goddesses for fertility, successful harvests, and the weather.

Knowing how our ancestors lived closely with Nature, relying on her for survival, it makes complete sense that they would have needed to mark the passage of time and the change of seasons, particularly the coming and going of the sun, the giver of light and life.

Ancient Monuments Aligning with the Sun

Adapting to the turning points in Nature would have been crucial to survival, which may explain why many ancient monuments were erected to align with the movements of the sun—the most famous being Stonehenge in Wiltshire, where approximately five thousand years ago standing stones were put up to frame the sunset at the winter solstice and sunrise on the summer solstice. Many ancient civilizations didn't have written languages and so their celebrations have been lost through the ages, but it is likely that people gathered at Stonehenge at the turning points of the year to conduct rituals and ceremonies as the seasons changed.

However, Stonehenge is not the only ancient site to align with the solstices. Bryn Celli Ddu in Anglesey, North Wales is a burial tomb that is illuminated by shafts of sunlight each year on the summer solstice; while in Ireland, the winter solstice sun lights up the 5,200-year-old passage tomb and chamber in Newgrange, thought to mark the beginning of a new year and a symbol of the victory of life over death. The same happens at Maeshowe in Orkney, Scotland.

Further afield, in Machu Picchu, Peru, the Temple of the Sun has windows positioned to capture sunlight so that it falls directly on to a ceremonial stone during the solstice. And, also in Machu Picchu, the ritual stone Intihuatana is positioned so that the sun stands directly above it on the equinoxes, creating no shadow at all.

At Angkor Wat in Cambodia, the sunrise on the spring and autumn equinoxes aligns directly over the central lotus tower, the peak of the main temple. In Mexico, the Pyramids of Chichen Itza were designed to create a light-and-shadow phenomenon on the equinox, which looks like a serpent. While in Egypt, the Karnak Temple aligns with the winter solstice.

There are so many examples of ancient sites and monuments that observe the turn of Nature's seasons and the movements of the skies, showing how our ancestors lived in alignment with and honored, celebrated, and revered the natural world around them.

The Wheel of the Year, as we know it today, has strong roots in Celtic culture and their celebrations of the cross-quarter festivals.

The Celts were tribal groups who lived in parts of western and central Europe in the late Bronze Age. Much of their culture and religion was closely tied to Nature, with a belief that the sacred could be found through her, and that everything was cyclical, repeating in a natural cycle of death and rebirth. The Druids, their religious leaders, communed between humanity and the gods, oversaw the rituals and sacrifices, made medicinal potions with plants, and interpreted the events of Nature.

The Celts had a deep connection to the natural world, believing that the divine manifested itself through Nature. Their gods and goddesses were therefore worshipped everywhere in Nature, from trees to mountains, lightning to wind, rocks to streams. They believed that certain natural sites, such as hills, individual, or groves, of trees and rivers held deep spiritual significance and were considered portals to the divine and the otherworld. Rituals, celebrations, and offerings to the gods and goddesses would happen in these special places, and they would be held in accordance with the cycles of Nature, the planets, the sun, and the moon. This was how they marked seasonal shifts and connected to the rhythm of the natural world around them.

The Celts celebrated the four fire festivals of Samhain, Imbolc, Beltane, and Lughnasadh, using them to dictate when to plant, plow, sow, harvest, fish, hunt, and rest. Feasts were had, rituals performed, crops planted and harvested, preparations made for the coming season, and the active and dormant phases of Nature were recognized. The gods and goddesses were paid tribute to, and festivities were focused on bringing the community together to give thanks and honor the cyclical nature of life and death and the gifts of each season.

Celtic culture and religion started to wane with the expansion of the Roman Empire, when many Celts scattered to more remote parts of Ireland and northern Britain. The Romans sought to shift the focus of religion to civil worship, and the sacred and divine were no longer considered to be found in Nature. So began the spiritual disconnection of people from Nature, changing their relationship to the natural world around them.

With the introduction of Christianity, many of the old traditions were lost and destroyed. Celtic gods were turned into saints and many of the Celtic celebrations became Christian festivals, their significance altering to suit the church.

The traditional calendar of the Wheel of the Year was more recently adopted by the neopaganism and Wiccan movements, who seek to reconnect back to Nature, goddess worship, and the seasons and cycles.

Bringing all 8 festivals—the 2 solstices, 2 equinoxes, and 4 cross quarter festivals—was first suggested by German author Jacob Grimm in 1853.

This was later picked up in the 1950's by Gerald Gardner, founder of modern day Wicca, and Ross Nichols, an academic and founder of the Order of the Bards, Ovates and Druids, and by the mid-1960's this was the accepted Wheel of the Year of witches.

In 1974, Aidan Kelly gave names to the festivals, drawing on Celtic inspiration for the cross-quarter festivals and Anglo-Saxon names for the solstices and equinoxes, which are still commonly used today.

MAKING THE WHEEL OF THE YEAR YOUR OWN

Many ancient cultures did not keep written records, and their traditions were handed down orally. This means that much of what we know today of the ancient ways is wrapped in myth, folklore, and speculation. Yet I also believe they are entrenched in our psyche—that, deep down, we know ourselves to be part of Nature, evolving with each of her turning points.

Any one of us, in any moment, can begin to live back in alignment with this natural flow to change our lives, reclaiming our connection to ourselves, creation, and the divine. It doesn't need to be a huge life overhaul, but simple little daily changes and rituals honoring the turn of the seasons will make a huge difference in our lives.

Each time the Wheel of the Year turns, it takes us into a new energy phase to work with, and although we don't rely on Nature for survival in quite the same way that our ancestors did, we can still invite the same ancient wisdom and guidance back into our modern-day lives to live with more meaning and purpose.

How often do you find that each month merges into the next, summer into winter and one year into the next? And before you know it, you realize you are still stuck where you were a year ago? Living in alignment with Nature and the Wheel of the Year means no longer doing this. Instead, you have regular opportunities to pause and check in with yourself. And it's in these moments of pause that you get to review your life, make any necessary Nature-inspired changes and move forwards into a new season with renewed clarity and purpose.

The Astrological Seasons

The astrological seasons are defined by the time the sun spends in each sign of the zodiac. As mentioned earlier, the sun doesn't move through the signs of the zodiac; this is an optical illusion created by the earth orbiting the sun.

As the earth moves around the sun from our viewpoint, the sun will appear to pass in front of the twelve different constellations/astrological signs of the zodiac through the year, spending approximately thirty days in each sign, known as seasons.

As the sun moves through each astrological season, it beams down the energy of that zodiac sign for us to embody and work with. This takes us on a year-long journey, enabling us to work with different energies, traits, lessons, and qualities:

- ARIES (21 March–19 April)—the trailblazer who helps you to get things started

- TAURUS (20 April–20 May)—grounds you and helps you to become aware of the wisdom of your body

- GEMINI (21 May–20 June)—unlocks the power of your mind and instigates change

- CANCER (21 June–22 July)—brings you home to yourself and helps you to embrace your emotions and intuition

- LEO (23 July–22 August)—connects you to your heart and shows you how to express yourself and shine

- VIRGO (23 August–21 September)—helps you to be present, make a plan and become aware of how you can be of service in the world

- LIBRA (22 September–22 October)—brings balance and harmony and asks you to look at all your relationships (including with yourself)

- SCORPIO (23 October–21 November)—takes you into your depths, demanding truth and transformation

- SAGITTARIUS (22 November–20 December)—leads you into adventure, opportunities, and exploration

- CAPRICORN (21 December–19 January)—desires discipline and focus, planning for the longer term

- AQUARIUS (20 January–18 February)—seeks freedom, revolution, and faith in where your journey is taking you

- PISCES (19 February–20 March)—brings spirituality, awakening, forgiveness, and endings to create a new beginning

The zodiac signs are broken down into three modalities—cardinal, fixed, and mutable, which is where they link to both the Wheel of the Year and Nature's seasons:

- CARDINAL SIGNS These begin each season and bring us the solstices and equinoxes: Aries starts spring, Cancer summer, Libra autumn, and Capricorn winter. Cardinal signs are the leaders, initiating new beginnings and making things happen.

- FIXED SIGNS These stabilize each season and bring us the cross-quarter festivals at the midway point of each one: Taurus stabilizes spring, Leo summer, Scorpio autumn, and Aquarius winter. Fixed signs are firm and dependable, anchoring us into the season and encouraging us to see things through.

- ♦ **MUTABLE SIGNS** These end each season: Gemini ends spring, Virgo summer, Sagittarius autumn, and Pisces winter. Mutable signs prepare us for change, transition, and transformation, helping us to move forwards and adapt to a new season.

Nature's Seasons

As Nature moves through each of her seasons, she inspires us, showing us how to blossom and bloom, grow, transform, let go, and be reborn. Living in alignment with Nature ensures that we too are constantly evolving, renewing, releasing, and growing—just as she does. It also means that, rather than pushing against the natural world around us, we live in rhythm with it, looking to it for support and inspiration.

When we begin to attune ourselves to the natural world around us and live in flow with its wisdom, our lives take on so much more meaning and flow.

Just like the astrological seasons, each of Nature's seasons brings different energy, lessons, and opportunities.

SPRING

Spring is the season of birth and growth, where much of Nature begins to blossom and bloom into life. What has been germinating beneath the surface begins to take physical form in the world as the sunnier days awaken the first flowers and leaves.

Light and warmth increase and there is something fresh in the air—a sense of expectancy, possibility, and opportunity. It feels like a new beginning after the darkness of winter.

Just as Nature is growing, she inspires us to do the same. Spring is the time to put new ideas, goals, and plans into action—to go back out into the world, fueled by the light and life appearing all around us, being playful and embracing the fresh, new energy and opportunities coming our way.

SUMMER

Summer is the season of abundance, when Nature is in full bloom, expansion and growth. The sun is at its peak, the days are at their longest and warmest, and everything is bursting with life. There is a sense of joy and happiness in the air, and it feels like opportunities are everywhere.

This is the time for us to be inspired by Nature, creating, developing and manifesting, bringing things fully to life. The longer days and peak energy of the sun's warmth offer the chance to be more productive and "out there" in the world, making things happen. This is the season for fun and adventure; for appreciating and enjoying life and everything that has grown in our lives over the previous few months.

AUTUMN

Nature now begins to shed, release, and let go—and this is where the harvest is gathered in preparation for winter. As the nights begin to shorten and the sun begins to fade, all around us are signs of slowing down and beginning to draw inwards.

Autumn inspires us to be grateful for all that we enjoyed over the spring and summer, and to begin to shed, release, and let go ourselves of all that we no longer need or want to take into winter with us. This is the season to give thanks for all we experienced over summer and to begin the preparations for winter. It is a time to nourish and nurture ourselves and bring things back into balance.

WINTER

At this, the darkest and coldest time of the year, Nature retreats within to pause and take stock. Everything is dormant, resting, and conserving energy. And just as Nature draws inwards, hibernating, she inspires us to do the same over the winter months.

This is the season for introspection, deep rest, and connecting with our inner worlds. It's in this quiet time of reflection that we get to learn the lessons from the year gone by and make any necessary changes within. It is when Nature dies, to be reborn come spring; and we too get to allow things we no longer need to die away, so that we can do things differently at our own rebirth in spring.

CHAPTER 3

The Moon Through the Seasons

The moon has long been a marker of the turn of the seasons, used by our ancestors to keep track of the passing year and when to plant, harvest, hunt, fish, and gather. Names were given to the moons based on the weather, behavior of animals and plants, and what was happening in Nature at the time, so that people knew what to expect and how to prepare.

I will give you details of the new and full moon that fall in each season as another way for you to embrace cyclical living and harness wisdom and guidance from the moon, as our ancestors did. You can read more about living in alignment with the magic of the moon and her cycles in my book *Lunar Living*, but here's a brief summary.

The moon is moving in constant cycles, going through eight different phases and every sign of the zodiac in approximately a month.

The lunar journey begins with the new moon, when the sun and moon are in the same place in the sky. (So the new moon will always fall in the same sign as the zodiac season we are in.)

♦ THE NEW MOON is a brand-new beginning, a chance to start over, and this is where we set intentions for what we want to create and invite into our lives. Over the next two weeks, as the moon waxes (gets bigger and brighter in the sky), she inspires us to go out there into the world to be seen, to shine, and to give all our energy, focus, and attention to our new-moon intentions. (I refer to the moon as "she" or "her" because the moon is the feminine energy of the universe that connects us to our inner world, intuition, and the call of our souls.)

♦ ON A FULL MOON the moon and sun are on opposite sides of the earth, and it is the light of the sun illuminating the moon's surface that gives us the full moon. This means that the full moon will always be in the opposite zodiac sign to the one that we are currently in. On a full moon we celebrate what we've achieved, consider what got in the way of us getting what we wanted and look at what we are ready to release. Over the next two weeks, as the moon wanes (gets smaller and smaller in the sky), she inspires us to turn inwards and do the healing and inner work required, so that we may let go of all that we no longer need and what-ever gets in the way.

NOTE: the dates of the new and full moon in each season will vary year on year, but you can find the dates of this year's moons on my website, kirstygallagher.com.

I will give you a brief insight and a mini moon ritual for the new and full moon for each season, so that you can harness her energies to deepen the sacred season. (If you enjoy the lunar work and want to make it part of your sacred-seasons practice, you can also check out *The Lunar Living Journal*, which will take you through a whole year of living with the moon with more in-depth information, journal prompts, and regular check-ins.)

The following are the names given to the moons (they were only given to full moons, as this is when the moon is most visible in the sky—she is not visible on a new moon); many of these names have Indigenous American roots, passed down through generations and around the world by early settlers:

♦ JANUARY—known as the wolf moon, as this was the time of year wolves were most vocal as they marked their territory, gathered for hunting and located each other; also known as ice, frost-exploding, or hard moon.

♦ FEBRUARY—known as the snow moon, as this was typically the time of year that saw the most snowfall; also known as hungry, black-bear, or storm moon.

♦ MARCH—known as the worm moon, as this was when earthworms would emerge, and their trails would appear in the thawing ground; also known as sap, crust, crow, or wind-strong moon.

♦ APRIL—known as the pink moon for the appearance of one of the first spring wildflowers (the wild ground phlox or grass pink); also known as egg, breaking-ice, fish, or budding moon of plants and shrubs.

- MAY—known as the flower moon for the abundance of flowers that come into bloom during this month; also known as hare, corn-planting, or leaf-budding moon.

- JUNE—known as the strawberry moon, as this was when the season reached its peak and ripe strawberries were gathered; also known as hot, blooming, or rose moon.

- JULY—known as the buck moon, as this was when male deer's antlers would begin to rapidly grow back after shedding; also known as thunder, hay, salmon, or half-way-summer moon.

- AUGUST—known as the sturgeon moon, as this was when these large fish, common to the great lakes, were caught; also known as red or grain moon.

- SEPTEMBER—known as the harvest moon, as this was when staple foods and crops were ready for gathering; also known as corn, barley, autumn, or falling-leaves moon. This moon is traditionally the full moon closest to the autumn equinox, which is usually in September, but can sometimes be in October. When this happens, September's moon is called the corn moon and October's would be the harvest moon.

- OCTOBER—known as the hunter's moon, as this was when game was fattened and most easily spotted for hunting; also known as travel or dying-grass moon.

- **NOVEMBER**—known as the beaver moon, as these animals were busy preparing to retreat into their winter dams; also known as frost or whitefish moon.

- **DECEMBER**—known as the cold moon, as this was the coldest and darkest time of the year, with everything in the grip of winter; also known as long-night, winter-maker, or mid-winter moon.

A Word on Calendars

Ancient calendars were based on the moon, and the word "month" comes from the same root as the word "moon." It seems that people have looked to the sky for meaning, purpose, and the passing of time for centuries.

Where the sun would have kept rhythm for a day and night, looking further ahead would have meant deferring to the moon. The most visible object in the sky, she would have helped people keep track of time, as she passed through each of her eight different phases over her (roughly) twenty-eight-day cycle—from no moon to full moon and back to no moon again.

Early lunar calendars were complicated, comprising twelve moon cycles, with a thirteenth month added in every two or three years to account for the fact that the lunar and solar cycles aren't the same in length.

The original calendar (dating back to 738 BC) started in March, and even though there were twelve months, only ten had names, as winter was a "dead" period when nothing happened. In fact, the spring equinox was celebrated by the British empire as the new year until 1752, showing how closely our ancestors tied their lives to the natural world.

Eventually, January and February were added to the end of the year, and then moved to the beginning, when it became the solar calendar as we know it today, with leap years.

CHAPTER 4

Connecting Back to Nature

At one time, we lived alongside Nature and were intrinsically attuned to her rhythm and flow. Our ancestors lived by the cycles of the sun and moon, rising at sunrise, being the most active during daylight hours, and resting when darkness fell. They sought the sacred and divine through Nature, adapted their lifestyles to the seasons and lived in harmony and flow with the natural world.

Over time, however, we moved to a more urbanized lifestyle, eventually turning our attention away from the natural world, toward our phones, computers, and TV screens. Today, we have completely lost touch with Nature; and, in doing so, we have lost a part of ourselves.

Yet, in truth, we are part of Nature. We are all made of stardust; nearly all the elements in our bodies were made in a star.

Sit with that for a moment. Close your eyes and feel it within you—that you are made of stardust. That within you, right now, are elements that were created billions of years ago in multiple star lifetimes. You are bits and pieces of star and cosmic dust. The human body is even said to contain traces of the Big Bang. The same energy source that created the entire universe and all of Nature also created you.

How can you think of yourself as separate from Nature now that you know this?

And I believe that the same universal life-force energy that moves through Nature, causing blooms to blossom, the tides to turn, and the leaves to shed, also moves through us, making our hearts beat and our hair and nails grow. I also believe that some part of us recognizes this when we spend time in Nature, and that's why we feel so good after doing so. Through Nature, we get to connect to that stardust part of ourselves; the infinite, expansive part—what I would call our souls.

Just like our ancestors did, we get to connect to the divine life-force energy moving through everything when we spend time in Nature. We are reminded that we are part of something way greater, and there is a guiding force in life if we choose to tune into it. We recognize part of ourselves in Nature and awaken that part of us that is connected to everything.

When we tune back into the natural world around us and begin to live with Nature, honoring her seasons and cycles, our lives change. We start to trust the journey of our souls and embrace life's natural unfolding. We adjust to a rhythm and flow that our bodies, our beings, our souls already know. No longer are we pushing, pulling, and struggling; instead, we get to live in flow with life and the natural world that we live in and are intrinsically a part of.

I truly believe that living back in alignment with the seasons and cycles of the natural world holds so many of the answers that we are all searching for. In fact, numerous bodies of research show that people who regularly connect with Nature experience better mood, improved attention span, lower stress levels, reduced anxiety, enhanced immune-system function, and higher empathy.[1]

In 1964, psychologist Erich Fromm first used the word "biophilia" to describe "the passionate love of life and all that is alive." The term was later used by Edward O. Wilson as a title for his 1984 work, in which it was defined as the innate human instinct to connect with Nature and other living beings.[2]

I believe that there is an ancient part of us that does once again seek to connect to Nature and other living beings, and this book is here to guide the way.

Let's consider just a few more of the things that you'll discover by living in connection with Nature.

How to Embrace Change

Did you know that the cells in our bodies replace themselves every seven to ten years? Just like Nature and the world around us, we are cyclical beings, our bodies in continual seasons and cycles, constantly regenerating, shedding and replacing.

But very often, we get stuck on our journey of life. We expect life to be linear, that things will be the same all day every day. As humans we cling, and we grip and we try to control and grasp on to things. But it's when we resist change or growth in this way, holding on to what we have outgrown and what is no longer

---

1 https://www.ncbi.nlm.nih.gov/pmc/articles/PMC4548093/
2 https://www.britannica.com/science/biophilia-hypothesis

working for us, that we become stagnant, stuck, and unhappy.

This is where we can turn to Nature for guidance. Nature moves in the rhythm of divine timing and knows that there is a reason and season for everything. She never resists change or forces growth. Nature understands cycles.

A wonderful example is when trees lose their leaves. You never see a tree clinging on to a leaf for fear there won't be another to take its place. It simply lets the leaves go, trusting that others will grow again in time.

How much easier life would be if we trusted and lived as Nature does. And we can. Living in alignment with Nature shows us that change is the only constant, and that each season is as beautiful as the last when we embrace it.

How to Honor Seasons

In our modern-day world, we have the notion that we should always be in full bloom. We celebrate being "on" all the time and fear the times of void or quiet. But in doing so, we never give ourselves time to rest, recover, and regenerate; nor do we pause to celebrate and look at how far we have come.

Nature teaches us how to slow down and rest, to draw our awareness inwards and take care of ourselves; that times of emptiness and hibernation are a vital part of life, to be honored and embraced, rather than resisted.

There are going to be seasons in your life when you are in full abundance, growth, and bloom, and others when you perhaps feel exhausted, or as though nothing is growing or happening. From my own experience, it's from these desolate times that I learn the most about me, and life. It's in the times of darkness that we, just like Nature, must look inwards for our strength and resilience to survive. Nature teaches us how to embrace the darkness and shadows of life, and that during these seemingly void times, we are growing from within, so that we can blossom into something even greater when that season of our lives comes around again.

Nature is living proof that "this too shall pass"; the light will follow the dark, the sun will rise again and, out of barren landscapes, the most beautiful blossoms and blooms will appear. And, when they do, Nature shows us how to celebrate and truly enjoy them, to grow and welcome all that life has to offer, no longer resisting the seasons, but recognizing them instead, and honoring where we are in our life's journey.

Our own life journey is mirrored in Nature—the evolutionary desire of our souls to flow and grow through cycles and seasons of death and rebirth, expansion and release. In this, Nature becomes our greatest teacher and inspiration.

When we embrace the seasons, of both Nature and our lives, we learn to enjoy them all—to take rest when required, to welcome the quiet times and to enjoy being in full growth and bloom when it's time.

How to Slow Down and Be Present

How often do we rush through life never pausing, stopping, or noticing? The present moment is all we ever have, but we miss it time and time again, always rushing to the next moment or spending time revisiting past ones.

Nature is only ever in the present moment. She is never looking back to what was or forwards to what is not yet here.

Turn your attention from your screen to the incredible world around you. Spend time in Nature and really *be* there. Gaze at the opening buds of a flower, place your hands and forehead against the trunk of a tree, listen to the sounds around you—the birds, the breeze, the leaves. Engage all your senses and allow Nature to show you how to be right here, right now—present, as she is.

How to Be All of Yourself

Nature teaches us how to love, accept, and be all of ourselves. You never witness a flower trying to dim and hide its beauty, or not want to come into full flower, worried what other flowers may say. Nor do grasses not grow to their tallest, or fruit trees worry about whether they'll bear the right fruit, or mushrooms that they aren't pretty enough, or buds that their blooms may not be up to scratch.

Nature is perfect, whole, and complete just as she is—and so are you. Everything in Nature knows its purpose and just expands into the full expression of whatever that is in perfect timing, knowing that what it has to offer is exactly what the world needs.

I believe that we too come into this world with our own unique expression, purpose, and offerings. We are part of the ecosystem of the world and, just like Nature, we have a purpose and a part to play just by being here—by being ourselves and who we came here to be.

How to Enjoy the Simple Things in Life

We are constantly seeking answers, happiness, and validation in the external material world, yet almost everything we need can be found in the natural world. In Nature, we can find the joy of connection, wonder, stillness, peace, and strength. Time in Nature doesn't cost a thing.

Nature doesn't need us to have the material things that the world tries to trick us into believing we require to belong and feel like we are enough.

In fact, think of five of the happiest times in your life, or the times when you felt most peaceful, connected, alive, or most like yourself. I'll bet that at least some of them involved Nature. Perhaps you watched a magical sunrise, had a jungle adventure, experienced solitude in the forest, took a frosty early-morning walk, or were immersed in the healing waters of the sea.

When you have your feet on the earth, the sun on your face, and fresh air in your lungs, you realize how little else you actually need to be happy and content.

CHAPTER 5

The Wisdom of Nature

I've always loved being in Nature. It's a place I go to for solace, solitude, inspiration, and to simply feel alive. In Nature, I'm able to more easily access my intuition and deeper wisdom, and I truly believe that the universe speaks to me through her.

Nature has always been one of my greatest teachers. Whenever I am in any doubt or need answers or guidance, I look to Nature for her wisdom, and she will hold, soothe, guide, and answer me.

I want to invite you too to develop a relationship with the world around you and turn to Nature for whatever you need. This book is a guide, but the ultimate teacher is Nature herself.

Observe the world around you—the world that you are part of. Walk in Nature every day and see how she is transforming and what she is teaching, guiding, and inspiring you to do. Search for parallels in your own life and notice how time in Nature makes you feel. Look to Nature and let her show you the way.

Here are just some of the lessons I have learned from Nature.

The Wisdom of Trees

Trees teach us about grounding and strength and provide a reminder to grow strong roots. Many have stood in the same place for hundreds, if not thousands, of years, witnessing the passing of time. They have seen it all, and we can turn to these ancient wisdom-keepers for guidance and answers whenever we need to.

Trees teach us about connection, too. Beneath the soil is a complex underground system which they use to communicate, warn each other of danger, and share nutrients. They teach us patience, yet also remind us of the beauty of letting go. They show us how to draw nourishment from the earth, while reaching our arms up to the skies.

HOW TO CONNECT WITH THE WISDOM OF TREES

Trees are living beings, and when we wrap our arms around them, we connect to their energetic vibration and can access their wisdom and power.

I know that the term "tree hugger" is often used for hippies, but hugging trees has been proven to release oxytocin, the hormone of love, trust, and bonding.[3] In fact, in Iceland, the forestry service encouraged tree hugging during the COVID-19 pandemic to overcome feelings of loneliness, even clearing pathways to make trees more easily accessible. But if hugging a tree feels like too much to begin with, try just placing your palm on a tree and feeling its energy, strength, support, and perhaps even its messages. Or sit

---

3 https://ridelikeaninja.com/2016/06/16/science-shows-hugging-trees-is-good-for-health/

with your back to its trunk and sink into its support.

Alternatively, you could go and "bathe" in the trees. Known as *shinrin-yoku*, forest bathing was first developed in Japan in the 1980s, following scientific studies carried out by the government.[4] The purpose was to offer an antidote to tech burnout and to inspire people to connect with the country's forests. Results showed that time spent among the trees boosted the immune system, lowered blood pressure and stress hormones, and improved sleep, concentration, and memory. So turn off your tech and head into the forest to wander among the trees and be present with the natural world. Feel the silence, presence, and power of the trees and let them inspire you.

The Wisdom of Water

Water teaches us to go with the flow, especially when we feel like we are struggling and swimming against the tide. It shows us how to trust, surrender, let go, and allow ourselves to be carried, like rivers to the sea. Water will always find a way, even if it is not obvious at first, teaching us to adapt, let go of rigid attachments and having to be a certain way, and never give up. Water is cleansing; the sea, rain, lakes, streams, and tears all help to wash away anything that we no longer need.

HOW TO CONNECT WITH THE WISDOM OF WATER

Few things will make you feel as alive and free as wild swimming, whether that's in the sea, a pond, or a lake. Not only does it get you closer to Nature, but it's been shown to release the feel-good hormones dopamine and serotonin, which increase feelings of

---

4 https://www.ncbi.nlm.nih.gov/pmc/articles/PMC5580555/

happiness and wellbeing, reduce inflammation in the body, stimulate the lymphatic system, and boost the immune system.[5]

But if you prefer to sit on the sidelines, you'll still benefit. Research by Richard Shuster, a clinical psychologist, showed that gazing at the ocean changes the frequency of our brain waves and, combined with the sound of the ocean waves, promotes feelings of deep relaxation.[6]

Waves are also often likened to our thoughts and emotions, so spend time watching them to see that nothing is permanent; it's all ever-changing. (And speaking of emotions, give yourself permission for a good cry whenever you need it. Crying has been proven to help release stress and emotional pain, restoring emotional balance and releasing feel-good chemicals.[7])

The Wisdom of the Earth

The earth holds and supports us, giving us a sense of safety, a place to land, arrive, and belong. It teaches us that we can only truly grow when our roots are nourished and planted deep, helping us to stay grounded, connected to something strong beneath us that will support us through times of challenge or change.

HOW TO CONNECT WITH THE WISDOM OF THE EARTH

Go barefoot on the earth as often as you can. Known as grounding or earthing, research has shown that when our bare feet (or any skin) come into direct contact with earth, we connect to its natural

---

5   https://www.ncbi.nlm.nih.gov/pmc/articles/PMC7730683/; https://www.newscientist.com/article/mg24933250-600-cold-water-swimming-what-are-the-real-risks-and-health-benefits/
6   https://www.nbcnews.com/better/health/what-beach-does-your-brain-ncna787231
7   https://www.health.harvard.edu/blog/is-crying-good-for-you-2021030122020

electrical charge, drawing free electrons into our bodies.[8] This has been shown to reduce inflammation, pain, and stress, and improve our energy, vitality, and sleep quality.[9]

You can take this a step further by imagining sending roots from the soles of your feet deep into the earth to immediately feel a sense of connection and belonging. Visualize with each inhale drawing energy, nutrients, and anything else you need up from the earth and through your body. With each exhale, imagine sending anything you no longer need down into the earth where it will be transmuted.

In times of real overwhelm, lie on the earth with your arms and legs wide. With each deep exhale, sink into the earth beneath you and feel a sense of surrendering into it, allowing yourself to be held and supported.

The Wisdom of the Sky

The sky reminds us of the infinite, expansive universe that we are all part of. I mentioned earlier that we are all made of stardust (see p. 39) and, for me, there is nothing more magical than seeing a skyful of glimmering stars—a reminder of where we came from. Let the night skies remind you that there is an ancient, unlimited, open part of you that has all the answers.

You may be aware of my love affair with the moon, but still, there is something breathtaking, mesmerizing, and awe-inspiring about seeing her hanging there in the sky. As she moves through her eight phases, she teaches us how to expand and grow, shine, and let go—

---

8   https://www.ncbi.nlm.nih.gov/pmc/articles/PMC4378297/
9   https://www.sciencedirect.com/science/article/pii/S1550830719305476

that there are times for doing and times for resting and taking care of ourselves.

The sun teaches us about endings and beginnings, offering us the opportunity to let go at the end of each day and welcome a new beginning at the start of the next. The sky, the moon, and the stars also teach us about connection. Wherever we are, we all look at the same sun, the same moon in the same phase in the same sky and we all come from the same stars. We are all always connected.

And let's not forget astrology: the study of the movements and patterns of the planets and stars, and how these influence earthly events. We have looked to the skies for centuries for guidance and answers, and I believe the same holds true today. Not only can we defer to the stars to make more sense of the world we are living in, but our own birth charts give us a powerful way to know, under-stand, and accept ourselves on a much deeper level.

HOW TO CONNECT WITH THE WISDOM OF THE SKY

Any time that you need to shift your perspective or feel lost in worries, look to the vast sky and realize that all the little things that concern you are so small in comparison to what is out there.

Stargazing reconnects you with Nature and that wise ancient part of you, reminding you that you are part of something much greater and that there is a whole other world out there, outside of what you see in your day-to-day life. Studies have suggested that stargazing can boost creativity, inspire awe, reduce stress, and make us kinder and more mindful.[10] Stargazing is best done on nights closer to a new moon (when there is no moon in the sky— see p. 34).

---

10 https://pureportal.coventry.ac.uk/en/publications/dark-nature-exploring-potential-benefits-of-nocturnal-nature-base-2

You can also connect to the wisdom of the skies by tracking the lunar cycles and learning more about the magic of the moon and how we can use her ancient wisdom in our daily lives (see my book *Lunar Living* for more about this). Gazing at the moon reminds me that we are part of something greater and there are guiding forces out there we can look to for answers, support, and ancient wisdom. Watch the moon nightly, as she transitions through her eight phases, and be inspired to grow and let go with her. Use the days of the dark moon (when there is no moon in the sky) to also withdraw from the world and take rest.

The daytime skies hold a lot of wisdom, too. We've likely all watched a sunrise or sunset and felt something stir within us. Witnessing these moments of beauty in Nature brings us into the present moment and moves us into deep gratitude for life and the blessing of another day: watch the sunrise to witness the beauty of another day—a whole 24 hours or 1,440 minutes ahead of you; watch the sunset as a reminder to let go with beauty and grace— that endings can be beautiful and it's ok to take a rest.

Try lying on your back and watching the clouds move across the skies as a reminder that everything passes. Meditation often uses the idea of thoughts being like clouds moving through the skies— imagine just letting them gently go without getting too attached to them.

And finally, if you have an interest in astrology, get your birth chart done (you can do this for free on my website, kirstygallagher.com). Your birth chart is a unique snapshot of the sky—the planets and stars—at the exact moment you were born; it's a journey of getting to know yourself like never before, giving you an insight into the lessons you came here to learn and who you came here to be.

Your Nature Wisdom

I recently asked on my Instagram (@kirsty_gallagher_) about what Nature teaches you and how you feel when you're in Nature. Here are just a few of the things you said…

"To slow down, to breathe, to be grateful, to appreciate beauty, life and the earth."

"Safe—like I've come home."

"Like you can forget all your troubles—even if it's just for a little while."

"She teaches me change is ok and to appreciate the little things."

"It reminds me that I am Nature, too."

"That everything has another chance at a new beginning—to start over again."

"Nature is always transitioning, and so are we. Some seasons go slower at times, and that's ok."

"Nature teaches me impermanence."

"I feel held in Nature—whatever I'm feeling I know I can just be."

"In Nature I feel supported, like a gentle hug."

"Calm, connected; the true version of me."

"Safe and inspired—like a spa for my nervous system."

"That nothing is stagnant; everything changes and grows."

"Feeds my soul. From the birds to the trees—it is a balm for my soul."

"Nature teaches me about rebirth."

"Makes me feel bathed in a strong sense of spirituality and purpose."

"I feel at peace; like I'm part of something much bigger than I understand."

"Strong and back to the essence of myself as creation."

"Nature reminds me it's ok to let go."

"To embrace change like the seasons. Go with the flow and always strive to grow."

"I feel free, yet connected and present in the moment."

"That we flow in cycles and should also honor our times for growth and hibernation."

"I feel a weight lifted off my shoulders as soon as I step into Nature and start to slow down."

"Alive, safe, strong, happy. I feel at home when I'm in Nature."

"I feel free! As if all my worries are gone, and life is beautiful once again."

"Nature is my anchor."

"Teaches me that nothing is permanent and that shedding and renewal are needed for growth."

"I feel home—finally somewhere I belong."

"Nature teaches me to be patient."

"Even after a storm, life goes on—even if it looks a little different than before."

"To slow down and notice the beauty around me every day."

"To be present. Everything changes and everything flows; appreciate the change."

"She reminds us of all that we once knew and have forgotten thanks to home and society conditioning."

"Nature is my connection. She lifts me, soothes me and makes me feel alive."

"Nature is my everything and gets me through every situation and feeling."

"Makes me forget my worries and lifts my spirits without fail. It's truly magical."

"It helps me appreciate the here and now."

"She teaches me peace. How to just be me and not compare myself to others."

PART II

The Practices

THE SACRED SEASON OF

Spring

START-OF-SPRING SEASON: 21 March–19 April—the sacred season for awakening (pp. 63–75)

MID-SPRING SEASON: 20 April–20 May—the sacred season for living in expectation (pp. 77–90)

END-OF-SPRING SEASON: 21 May–20 June—the sacred season for change and growth (pp. 91–100)

CHAPTER 6

Start-of-spring Season —the Sacred Season for Awakening

DATES: 21 March–19 April

WHEEL-OF-THE-YEAR CELEBRATION: spring equinox, approx. 21 March

ZODIAC SEASON: Aries

MOONS THIS SEASON: Aries new moon and Libra full moon

REFLECT THIS SEASON ON: what wants to awaken within you and begin to grow and come to life.

LOOK OUT IN NATURE FOR: flowers beginning to bloom, birds beginning to sing, and butterflies, bats, and bees beginning to emerge.

The start-of-spring season brings us the spring equinox, the start of the astrological new year and the season when Nature comes back to life.

This marks the beginning of the outer phase of the Wheel of the Year, when we take all we learned from our winter hibernation and time in the darkness and use it to determine what we want to create moving forwards.

All around us new life is emerging. Trees and flowers are starting to bloom, the sun is making more of an appearance and there is freshness in the air. The days are growing longer and lighter, and it's now that we shake off the darkness of winter. This is a time of hope and awakening and feeling into all that's possible for us.

Just as Nature is beginning to stir and awaken, you will find the same is happening within you. Nature is telling you that it's time to create, shine, and come back to life. You will feel a natural desire to move back out into the world, make things happen, and bring dreams and desires to life.

This season marks the start of the astrological new year, as the sun moves into Aries and brings the opportunity to "start over." The traditional new year has never really resonated with me. I find it difficult to set intentions and resolutions and visualize the year ahead when it's cold and dark and the world feels like it's still hibernating and sleeping. Life becomes very challenging when we push against Nature in this way, which is why many resolutions fail and we don't see things through. It makes so much more sense to do this at the spring equinox, when the world is waking up and everything around us is springing to life; so I treat the spring equinox as my new year, and this is when I set intentions and the journey of my year really begins.

A sacred pause

As you enter this new growth cycle, pause to reflect on how far you have come since the beginning of the traditional year and whether you are where you thought you'd be three months into the year. The likelihood is that many of us won't have got that far in the first few months of the traditional new year. But we're not meant to. Nature was still inward, resting and dormant, with nothing growing.

But now, especially if the traditional year hasn't quite started out how you wanted it to, you've got a second chance at a new beginning—this time with Nature and the world all around you on your side. So now is the time to consider what you are truly ready to welcome into your life.

JOURNAL PROMPTS FOR THE SACRED PAUSE

♦ Has the traditional year started how you wanted it to and why?

♦ Where are you ready for new beginnings in your life?

♦ What do you now want to create, grow, and bring to life?

Start-of-spring Altar

If you already have an altar, give it a spring clean.

Yellow and green are the main colors associated with spring, so decorate your altar with a cloth and/or candle in these colors, or something bright that represents the new beginning that Nature is offering us.

Decorate your altar with catkins or pussy willow or spring flowers like primroses and tulips, especially ones that are in bud, so you can watch as they open to life.

Add symbols of fertility and growth; eggs and hares are often associated with spring, but you may also add images or symbols of what you want to grow in your own life.

Start-of-spring Daily Rituals

Embrace these daily rituals to help you connect to the essence of this season and Nature's guidance.

OPEN TO RECEIVE

At the beginning of each day, open your arms and heart wide open and spend a few moments welcoming in new beginnings and opportunities. Feel as though you are opening yourself up to receive everything coming your way.

SYMBOLICALLY START OVER

Every morning, journal on how you can "start over today." This is a beautiful practice to help to let go of yesterday and forgive the past, and to see each day as a brand-new opportunity to create change and go after what you want.

MOVE MORE

With the lighter mornings and evenings, start to move more—whether that is a five-minute yoga practice, a morning dance or shake, or just getting out into Nature for a walk in the fresh air. Ultimately, do what feels good for you and watch your increased energy, as you awaken your body into spring.

Crystals for the Start of Spring

♦ CARNELIAN A powerful crystal, packed with life-force energy and fertility, carnelian will help you to work with the expansive, fertile energies that the spring brings to reach for what you want. As well as helping to raise your sense of self-worth and boost your confidence, carnelian also brings the courage to follow opportunities and spring into spring.

♦ MOSS AGATE Strongly connected to Nature, this is the perfect crystal companion as you move into a new season and see the signs of life all around you. Moss agate inspires and encourages new growth, supporting you in fresh starts and new goals and dreams.

Affirmations for the Start of Spring

♦ "Every day in every way my life gets better and better."

♦ "I move forwards with ease."

♦ "I welcome new beginnings into my life."

Ways to Work with Aries Season

Aries, as the first sign of the zodiac, begins and initiates, bringing a trailblazing energy to get things started. It is inspiring, courageous, fiery, and passionate, and under the influence of Aries energy, you will feel fearless—as though anything you set your mind and heart to is possible.

As the pioneer of the zodiac, Aries will bring a huge burst of energy and help to move you into uncharted territories to explore new ways of making things happen. If you tap into this Aries energy, you'll find your self-belief game is strong and that you have self-motivation levels that even your inner saboteur will struggle to contain.

USE ARIES SEASON TO...

♦ ...MAKE A FRESH START. As the beginning of the astrological year, this season is like a clean slate, so use it to start over. Look at areas of your life that need some fresh, new energy or where you want to begin again. Remember, it's never too late.

♦ ...GO FOR WHAT YOU WANT. Write down everything you have been putting on hold for the last year (or ten years!). Review your list, and whether there is anything on there that you want to let go of. Once you're clear on exactly which things you still want, set some deadlines and small monthly targets of how you will start to go after them.

♦ ...TRY SOMETHING NEW. This is also the season to try something new. Whether that's a new business venture, hobby, or habits and beliefs, get out of your comfort zone and follow a new adventure.

Start-of-spring Moons

The start-of-spring season brings us the Aries new moon and Libra full moon.

THE ARIES NEW MOON

As the first of the astrological year, the Aries new moon brings a new perspective, helping you to see a way forward and to take charge of your life.

This new moon will help you to follow your instincts, impulses, and intuition, and see past the nagging voice of doubt, so that you may instead believe in yourself and your passions and calling.

Aries helps you to tune profoundly into your heart and soul, and align with your deepest guidance, wisdom, truth, and purpose. Use this moon to tune into what is stirring, wanting to awaken within you and be brought to life.

Mini new-moon ritual

Under this new moon, set intentions for the next lunar year: what do you want your next chapter to be? Write it down in as much detail as you can, and then, as you move into a new season, ensure that your thoughts, words, beliefs, and actions all mirror what you want.

THE LIBRA FULL MOON

As the sign of balance, the Libra full moon comes along to bring you back into balance and alignment, and heal your relationship with yourself and others.

This full moon is going to help you to find equilibrium between who you were and who you are becoming. She will help you to realize where you are repeating cycles, keeping yourself and your life out of balance, and what needs to be released from the scales of your life to make room for the new beginnings that await you with the start of spring.

Mini full-moon ritual

Journal on where in your life you feel most out of balance, what keeps you stuck and unable to get things off the ground, or what you keep repeating that prevents you from moving forwards. What do you need to let go of to move on fully?

How to Connect with Nature and Her Wisdom

Spend some time observing all the new beginnings around you in Nature. Look at the flowers starting to bloom and the first signs of buds and shoots on the trees. Nature is showing you how to unfurl and come back to life.

Get outside every day (first thing, if you can), and feel the new life in the fresh spring air. Breathe in the creativity and growth that surround you. As you breathe out, let go of anything that feels stagnant or sluggish. Feel it in the air—that new things are coming.

One of the most beautiful symbols of this season of awakening is that many birds begin to return and start their morning chorus, signaling that lighter mornings are coming. Wrap up and head outside about half an hour before dawn to be treated to a concert from Nature like no other. Listen to the sounds and imagine they are messages just for you. What might those messages be?

The Spring Equinox

♦ DATE CELEBRATED: approximately 21 March

♦ ALSO KNOWN AS: Ostara or the vernal equinox

Our ancestors would have used the spring equinox to mark the return of the sun after a long, dark winter. It was a celebration of rebirth, life, and growth, holding the promise of new beginnings, as everything in Nature started to come back to life.

The spring equinox is associated with Ostara/Eostre, the Germanic goddess of the dawn, who represents fertility, renewal, rebirth, and awakening, and is responsible for bringing in spring. Her symbols were the egg, which contains the full potential of new life, and the hare, known for its fertility.

Legend goes that the animal kingdom gathered for the arrival of the goddess and each wanted to give her a gift. The hare had nothing of value, and so gave her all that he did have—an egg, which he decorated for her. The goddess saw his true kindness and spirit in the gift and declared the hare as her special animal. Another legend has it that Ostara found a bird almost frozen to death and rescued it by transforming it into a rabbit, who had the ability to lay colored eggs.

Ostara/Eostre later became Easter, which is celebrated on the first Sunday following the first full moon after the spring equinox (also known as the hare moon), with both the egg and the Easter bunny continuing to be symbols of this celebration.

SPEND THE SPRING EQUINOX WITH YOUR SOUL

The spring equinox brings us the first day of spring. All around you in the air is the promise of longer days, warmth and sunshine. There is a feeling that something magical is waiting just around the corner—an inner stirring that tells you to uncover some of the dreams that you have hidden during the hibernating winter months.

The spring equinox is all about positive life changes, new beginnings, following opportunities, initiating creative ventures, planning adventures, and looking to the future.

Just as Nature is now fully emerging from hibernation and shaking off winter, so are you. It's time for you to shine your light— no more hiding away or playing small; it's time to awaken who you are and embrace life with your arms and heart wide open.

See this as a time that's just bursting with new growth and life to help you move forwards to where you want to be. Tune into the fertile, sparkly energy of spring to begin to bring the seeds of your intentions, hopes, and dreams to life.

SPRING-EQUINOX RITUALS

Set time aside in the days around the spring equinox to dedicate to these ritual practices and make the most of this seasonal transition.

Set some spring intentions

The whole world is now filled with fertile energy and growth that you can use to grow your own ideas, hopes, and dreams. Decide what you want the spring season to bring for you and then set some intentions to help you get there.

A beautiful ritual is to set your intentions on some seeds. Whisper all your hopes and dreams into the seeds, then plant them and watch as they—and your dreams—bloom and grow.

Spring clean

With all the fresh cleansing spring energy that's in the air, this is the perfect time to spring clean your body, mind, emotions, and your home. It's said that your outer world reflects your inner one, so look around you: is there clutter everywhere or things shoved into the back of cupboards? What are you holding on to that is old and outdated and you no longer need?

Begin a meditation practice to clear and cleanse your mind, too. Let go of any old beliefs and emotional ties that hold you back.

Move your body more. Eat more healthy-living foods that nourish you. Start anew and go into this season with a fresh, clean spring in your step.

Find balance in your life

Day and night are of equal length on the spring equinox, so this is a great time to take a life review and make sure that you are as "in balance" as Nature. How is your work/home life balance? Do you give too much energy away to people who are never there when you need the support in return? Do you allow yourself enough time out for you? Do you prioritize your own needs as much as you do others'?

Take an honest look at all areas in your life. What do you need to let go of, and what do you need to invite in more of? Find ways that you can create more equilibrium, so you can blossom and grow into spring a happier, healthier, and more grounded and balanced you.

SPRING-EQUINOX JOURNAL PROMPTS

- Where do you feel most out of balance in your life right now?

- How have you been playing small, and how are you now ready to shine?

- What is stirring within you, wanting to be brought to life?

- What change/s do you want to make in your life as you emerge into spring?

- If you could allow one thing to burst into life right this moment, what would that be?

- What qualities and beliefs do you want to embody and allow to grow within you over spring?

Sacred Season Made Simple

Nature is inspiring you to awaken and come back to life and move back out into the world to make things happen.

Reflect on how far you have come since the beginning of the traditional year, and whether you're where you want to be.

Use the fiery go-getter energies of Aries season to take first steps and start to make things happen in your life.

The spring equinox will help you to find balance in your life, as you move into the season of new beginnings.

A moment of reflection

What have you learned about this season, and how can you apply it to your own life? How are you being called to awaken and emerge, and how can you answer the call of what is stirring within you? What can you do to create more balance in your life and where do you need to start over?

Reflect on the last season; did you do what you committed to doing?

This season I commit to:

_____

_____

_____

_____

CHAPTER 7

Mid-spring Season— the Sacred Season for Living in Expectation

DATES: 20 April–20 May

WHEEL-OF-THE-YEAR CELEBRATION: Beltane, 1 May

ZODIAC SEASON: Taurus

MOONS THIS SEASON: Taurus new moon and Scorpio full moon

REFLECT THIS SEASON ON: allowing yourself and your dreams to begin to grow into their full potential.

LOOK OUT IN NATURE FOR: birds nesting and feeding their young, bluebell woods, hawthorn blooming, and cuckoos calling.

Mid-spring brings us Taurus season and Beltane, the cross-quarter festival that celebrates the peak of spring.

All around us is the feeling of expectation and growth as earth energy is at its strongest and Nature at her most active, busy growing into its full potential.

Flowers are everywhere, the earth is lush and green, and there is a sense that Nature is virile, fertile, and celebrating being alive. We too will feel this same alive, fertile energy within us, calling us to allow ourselves and our dreams to grow into all that they can become.

Nature is inspiring us to uncover the full promise that lives within us and celebrate the creative life-force energy flowing through everything.

We now take our spring-equinox intentions and start to embody them, bringing them to life using the fertile, creative energy of Nature to help us to come into full bloom.

This is the season of joy, happiness, aliveness, and celebration. Whatever brings the most amount of happiness, freedom, and joy into your life—do more of that.

A sacred pause

Take a sacred pause here to review what makes you feel most happy, purposeful, and most like your true self, and what you have to offer the world just by being you.

Look at where you're not allowing yourself to grow and where you hold yourself back from all that you are capable of, or what parts of your life don't feel like they allow the full expression of you.

JOURNAL PROMPTS FOR THE SACRED PAUSE

◆ Are you doing enough of what makes you feel most alive, passionate, purposeful, and most like you?

◆ What gifts do you have to offer the world?

◆ Where do you limit yourself in life?

Mid-spring Altar

The colors of Beltane are red, silver, white, and green.

Add to your altar symbols of things that represent your passions and whatever brings you most joy. Let it be a celebration of your life and all that you are creating and inviting in.

Add symbols of love to your altar—whether that's self-love, the love you already have in your life, or the kind that you are ready to welcome into it. Place a list of everything that you most love about yourself and your life on your altar and read it daily.

Yellow flowers are a symbol of Beltane, as is hawthorn, and you may also add symbols of the sun and fertility.

Mid-spring Daily Rituals

Embrace these daily rituals to help you connect to the essence of this season and Nature's guidance.

VISUALIZE YOUR LIFE

Begin a daily visualization practice whereby, for a few minutes a day, you visualize all that you want, dream of, and desire coming to life. See it as though it is already here. How would that feel? How would your life change? Embody this feeling and start to live as though what you want is already here.

LIVE IN EXPECTATION

Expect that all that you want is coming to you, and don't doubt it. Look around you at Nature in its growth phase—Nature doesn't doubt whether the leaves will unfurl or the blossoms will bloom. She just expects it to happen and allows it to do so with perfect timing. Try living in a state of expectation that what you want is coming at any moment, too.

OPEN YOUR HEART TO RECEIVE

At the sacred season to welcome in not only more love, but also all that you desire, you need to make sure that you are open to receiving it all. Each day, place your hands over your heart and ask it how it feels. Turn your awareness toward your heart and listen to what it wants to share. Soothe any hurts or pain your heart may be feeling, hold yourself through any grief and, when you are ready, start to open your heart to receive again. Breathe into your heart and feel it expand and open beneath your hands.

Crystals for Mid-spring

♦ ROSE QUARTZ The crystal of love, rose quartz will help you with self-love, deepening love and welcoming in love, as well as connecting you with pleasure, passion, fertility, and joy.

♦ CLEAR QUARTZ Known for its high vibrations and ability to amplify, clear quartz is wonderful for helping you to bring your manifestations and intentions to life.

Affirmations for Mid-spring

♦ "I am worthy and deserving of all that I desire."

♦ "I expect the very best from life."

♦ "I am open to receive."

Ways to Work with Taurus Season

After the high energy of Aries season, the first earth sign of the zodiac comes along to help you slow down and connect deeply with yourself.

Taurus is practical, reliable, and resourceful—a natural problem-solver who can make any dream or idea come to life. This season will help you to ground what you started in Aries season, giving it deep roots, so that it can grow into life.

Taurus connects you with the magic and wisdom of the earth, seasons and cycles. This season is here to teach you that everything you need is already within you; you just need to go inwards and listen.

This is also the season for deep work on your self-worth. You are never going to be able to create what you want without believing that you are worthy and deserving of it. Remember that Nature doesn't doubt whether the seed will grow into what it's meant to become; you need to have the same faith and trust that the dreams and desires planted within you can grow, too.

USE TAURUS SEASON TO...

♦ ...GROUND YOUR DREAMS IN REALITY. Think about what you can practically do each day to take you closer toward what you want, then do it. Don't leave your dreams to just float about in the ether; this is the time to take practical steps toward making them real.

♦ ...LOVE YOURSELF. Begin a self-love practice. Journal each day on what you love about yourself, what you're doing well, and why you can have faith in yourself. This is the season to start to love, trust, and believe in yourself fully and completely.

♦ ...SLOW DOWN AND GO INWARDS. Start a daily meditation practice to help you find a strong inner foundation. Set a timer for 5–10 minutes and focus your awareness on your breath, allowing it to guide you into yourself. Take note of any insights or answers that come to you during this quiet time.

Mid-spring Moons

The mid-spring season brings us the Taurus new moon and Scorpio full moon.

THE TAURUS NEW MOON

The Taurus new moon comes along to help you slow down, get present and grounded, and find your roots. Taurus wants you to find stability and security that come not from anything external, but from deep within—from standing in your own truth and power, and from knowing, trusting, and connecting with who you truly are.

Being all about self-care, Taurus will show you how to put yourself first. If this is something you struggle with, then this is the moon for you to find the self-worth and self-love that will help you do it.

Mini new-moon ritual
Have a day or evening of self-care over this new moon and do things just for you and just because they feel good. Notice how you feel about self-care and whether you struggle to prioritize yourself. Make a commitment to do one thing for you every day over the waxing moon.

THE SCORPIO FULL MOON

Intense is a word that you hear a lot around this full moon. But I'd also love to give you the words "transformational" or "game changer" —because that's what this full moon always is. And I'll also give you the word "emotional," because this moon is an emotional ride, but one which takes you toward your soul's path and what you ultimately want in your life.

Under the illuminating light of the Scorpio full moon, you're able to clearly see where you can no longer keep doing what you've been doing, what emotional attachments or relationships in your life are unhealthy, where you are continuing to behave in ways that are no longer in alignment with what you say you want and ways in which you are still operating from old, subconscious programming or fears.

Mini full-moon ritual

One of the symbols of Scorpio is the phoenix, who asks you to throw all you no longer need on to the metaphoric flames so that it can be transformed, renewed, and born again into something new.

To honor this, create your own burning ritual under this full moon. Write down all that you wish to release—anything that's been holding you back, your doubts, fears, and all that you no longer want or need. Set the paper alight and drop it into a fireproof dish (please be safe!) feeling the fire burn away all that you want to let go of.

How to Connect with Nature and Her Wisdom

Notice how alive and fertile everything is in Nature on this cusp between spring and summer. Spend time watching bees darting between flowers to pollinate, the birds busy nesting and attracting a mate, the cherry blossom bursting, the ponds coming to life. Let Nature show you how to enjoy life and be open to receiving all the goodness in the world.

Head into ancient woodland to see the spectacular spring sight of carpets of bluebells covering the forest floors. As bluebells spend most of the year as a bulb underground, only appearing for a few weeks, they are a sure sign that spring is in full swing. As you wander among them, let these flowers teach you about timing, patience, and creating the right conditions for growth. Just be careful not to step on them, as it can take five to seven years for a bluebell patch to develop, and they take a lot of time to recover if damaged—a good lesson regarding our impact as we walk through life and a reminder to tread mindfully and lovingly.

Beltane

- ◆ DATE CELEBRATED: 1 May

- ◆ ALSO KNOWN AS: Beltaine or Beltain

Beltane is one of the four great fire festivals and was traditionally a celebration of life, the first signs of summer, the fertility of the land and people, and the promise of the light and growth to come.

Beltane is translated as bright fire, and communities would build fires to symbolize the growing power of the sun and to purify, cleanse, and renew after the dark months of winter. It was traditionally celebrated on the night of the full moon at the end of April/beginning of May or the first full moon after the hawthorn tree came into blossom.

The sacred union of Mother Earth and the Green Man, the Oak

King and the May Queen, or the horned god and the fertile goddess was celebrated and acted out by villagers for fertility. Couples spent the night outdoors making love and jumped the fire to pledge commitment to each other. Many traditions also honored the battle between the Queen of Winter and the May Queen, who awoke from her winter's sleep and banished the Queen of Winter for six months, so that the earth could become fertile and abundant once more.

A village girl would have been chosen to be crowned as the May Queen and, alongside a May King, lead the procession and celebrations, which included dancing around the maypole to represent the joining of male and female energies and the joy of new life.

As with many pagan festivals, Beltane was renamed (as May Day), with many of the same traditions being celebrated, if in a slightly different sense.

SPEND BELTANE WITH YOUR SOUL

Beltane celebrates spring magic. It is a time of fertility and growth, love and joy, sexuality and sensuality, the coming together of the masculine and feminine creative energies in all of us, and, most of all, abundance and happiness.

This turning of the season is the peak of spring and welcomes in the coming summer and the world coming alive. Everything in Nature is bursting with fertility, life, growth, power, and potential—and the same is true for you.

From this moment to the summer solstice is the peak energy time of the Wheel of the Year to manifest, create, and bring to life what you want.

BELTANE RITUALS

Set time aside in the days around Beltane to dedicate to these ritual practices and make the most of this seasonal transition.

Welcome and celebrate love

Beltane is the festival of love, so celebrate it. Traditionally, this was the time of handfastings (an ancient union ritual for couples— similar to a modern-day engagement) and vows, coming together in love and trust and commitment. If you are in a relationship, take some time this season to celebrate and enjoy your love, making a commitment to connect and spend quality time together. If you are looking for love, this could be the perfect time to welcome it in: write down all that you want from a partner and relationship, going into as much detail as you can; place your list under a candle on your altar and, each day, light it to welcome this love into your life. Spend a few moments feeling and visualizing the love that you want and opening yourself to welcome it in. Then blow out the candle and imagine sending your love-filled intentions out into the world. You could even keep a piece of rose quartz on top of your love list on your altar or whisper your intentions to your rose quartz, then carry it around with you, so that it can help love to find its way to you.

Review your spring-equinox intentions

Look back to six weeks ago (see p. 72) and the intentions you set yourself—how close or far away do they now seem?

This is a good opportunity to check in with whether you're giving your intentions the desired focus and energy they need and giving your time, energy, and attention to things that are going to get results. You may choose to refocus your direction, alter your intentions a little based on how you've grown over the last few weeks, and conceive a new project, idea, or something that you've been thinking about for a long time.

If there are any fears or anything that holds you back, write them down and then use the fire of Beltane to burn not only the paper, but all those fears and worries with it.

Visit a hawthorn tree

Viewed as a symbol of fertility, love, hope, and healing, the hawthorn tree has long been associated with ancient Beltane traditions. People would tie colored ribbons or pieces of cloth to a hawthorn —also known as the wishing tree—to represent their wishes.

If you choose to leave a wish, make sure that it's biodegradable or that you remove it afterward (you could then place your wish ribbon on your altar and meditate holding it every day). You could also gather some hawthorn for your altar and tie your wish around this, especially since superstition says that Beltane is the only day that you're allowed to disturb a hawthorn.

Otherwise, meditate with the hawthorn tree to open and heal your heart, and bring fertility, protection, and spiritual growth. Whisper your wishes to it, seek its guidance and wisdom, and allow the magic to unfold.

BELTANE JOURNAL PROMPTS

♦ What do you want to create, manifest, and bring to life during these fertile months?

♦ What three things do you need to be doing now, during this period of growth, to make these things happen and ensure that you will be able to reap the rewards come autumn?

♦ Are you truly open to receiving all that you desire, and all that the universe wants to bring? How can you open yourself up more to receiving what you want?

♦ How can you fall more in love with yourself and your life?

♦ How are you nurturing your dreams?

♦ What fears are holding you back?

Sacred Season Made Simple

Nature is inspiring you to begin to grow into your full potential and bring your dreams to life.

Reflect on your spring-equinox intentions and whether what you are doing now will bring the required results.

Use the fertile energy in Nature all around you, and the self-love and self-care energy from Taurus season to believe that you are worthy and deserving of all that you want.

Beltane will help you to manifest, create, and bring to life what you want.

A moment of reflection

What have you learned about this season, and how can you apply it to your own life? How are you being called to grow and expand, and where do you need to believe in yourself a bit more? What can you do to begin to bring your hopes and dreams to life?

Reflect on the last season; did you do what you committed to doing?

This season I commit to:

_____

_____

_____

_____

CHAPTER 8

End-of-spring Season— the Sacred Season for Change and Growth

DATES: 21 May–20 June

WHEEL-OF-THE-YEAR CELEBRATION: none

ZODIAC SEASON: Gemini

MOONS THIS SEASON: Gemini new moon and Sagittarius full moon

REFLECT THIS SEASON ON: any changes that need to be made in your life for you to be able to grow into your full potential.

LOOK OUT IN NATURE FOR: baby birds taking their first flight, flowers in full bloom, and shrubs, bushes, hedgerows, and trees exploding into life.

The end of spring brings us change-loving Gemini season, helping us to prepare to move into a brand-new Nature season.

Nature begins to shift into the last phase of spring growth and transformation, as summer begins to beckon. It's now clear what is growing in Nature—things are no longer buds and shoots or hiding under the ground; rather, they are bursting into their full potential for all to see. And this season wants the same for you.

It's time to get really clear on who you can be when you grow into your fullest potential and what you can offer to the world just by being you. This is the season to begin to bring to life all that you want and to do anything needed to help you to get there. See it as a last growth spurt in which to make changes that will ensure that your summer will be filled with even more happiness, abundance, and all that you want your life to be. Yes, growth and change are sometimes uncomfortable but, as you can see in Nature right now, it's so worth it.

Days are getting noticeably lighter and warmer, with the most hours of daylight and the anticipation of summer carried on the warm breeze, calling us forwards and preparing us to get out there in the world.

Both we and Nature are shifting up an energetic gear, preparing for the busyness, expansion, and abundance that summer will bring.

A sacred pause

Reflect on what stops you from growing, changing, and reaching your full potential. Look at any changes you know you need to make in your life, so as to be who you want to be and have what you want, and why you aren't making them. Are you afraid of change and what it will mean? Are you afraid to shine and bloom, or of what other people will think and say if you do? Where do you stay small and in the shadows, not reaching for all that you can be, holding yourself back over and over again?

Look around you. Flowers don't worry about what other flowers think; they simply bloom into their full beauty with no comparison, no holding back—just an unfolding into all that they can be. Be inspired by the flowers in Nature to make the changes you know you need to make to grow.

JOURNAL PROMPTS FOR THE SACRED PAUSE

- Where in your life do you feel stagnant, stuck, and as though you are not growing?

- Where and how do you most hold yourself back in life?

- What changes are you aware you need to make and how are you going to begin to make them?

End-of-spring Altar

Fill your altar with all the colors of spring (green, pink, yellow, and purple) and spring flowers in full bloom. Add images or anything that represents all that you want to grow into and become, and what you want to bring into your life.

Find a picture that represents you at your very happiest and most alive, and look at it daily as a reminder of you in your full potential. Perhaps ask friends and family what they most love about you and keep a list of these things on your altar as a reminder of what others see in you.

End-of-spring Daily Rituals

Embrace these daily rituals to help you connect to the essence of this season and Nature's guidance.

PUT PEN TO PAPER

This is the perfect season to try journaling. If you've never done it before, you may simply commit to writing one or two pages a day of whatever comes into your mind or what you are feeling. If you do already have a journaling practice, perhaps try it specifically for any issues you are facing, life areas you are struggling with, or emotions you are experiencing to see if you can get to some deeper answers or clarity. Journaling is a powerful route to self-discovery, and by committing to it daily you will learn so much about yourself.

SAY A LITTLE PRAYER

Gemini is ruled by Mercury, the planet of communication, making this the perfect season to find your voice and use the power of prayer. The word "prayer" has different connotations for different people, but I pray every day and see it as me asking the universe for help with what I need. Say a little prayer every day giving thanks, asking for any guidance and support you need, and letting the universe know just what you want. Your words have power; see what happens when you start to use them.

SEE THE SIGNS

I believe that the universe is always speaking to us and giving us signs, so this season start to notice them. It may be seeing repeating numbers, hearing about the same thing multiple times in a day, white feathers, animal visitors, or anything that feels meaningful or symbolic to you. Journal on what you feel the signs mean for you, and all that is unfolding and growing in your life as you begin to pay attention. Remember to say thank you and, most importantly, act on any signs that you are receiving. So if you are getting the nudge to call someone, make that call; or if you hear about the same thing multiple times, look into it.

Crystals for the End of Spring

♦ MALACHITE The crystal of change and transformation, malachite will help you to grow and move forwards in life, clearing limiting beliefs and embracing change. Just be prepared—because when you invite malachite into your life, change is coming.

♦ FLUORITE This crystal's name comes from the Latin word "flux," which means to flow or something that continually changes, making this the perfect crystal for this season of change. Fluorite helps to cut through confusion, bringing clarity and helping you to find your own flow.

Affirmations for the End of Spring

♦ "I embrace change."

♦ "I notice and follow the signs."

♦ "I am growing into all that I can become."

Ways to Work with Gemini Season

Taurus season helped us to get grounded and lay strong and firm roots and foundations. Now we shift into change-loving Gemini to help us to put things into action and move forwards. If you've been feeling that you need to make changes in your life, this is the season for it.

Gemini season helps you to prepare for change, not only in the seasons, but also in you. It brings ideas, inspiration, and enthusiasm, and an insatiable curiosity to explore all your different options and open yourself up to new ideas, opportunities, and ways of doing and being.

Gemini season will help you to seek out all the connections, tools, information, wisdom, and energy you need to grow toward your full potential and make any necessary changes. Lean into change this season and work with the energies, rather than trying to fight against them. You are being well supported by Nature right now.

USE GEMINI SEASON TO...

♦ ...MAKE CHANGES. If you've known for a while that things need to be shaken up, this is the time to do it. You may start with simple daily changes in your routines, having that hard conversation or finally taking that leap.

♦ ...GATHER WHAT YOU NEED. This is the time to gather anything you need to help you get to where you want to go. Do you need to ask for help, be more proactive, put yourself out there more, or study and gain a qualification? Whatever you need to move forwards and make a change, this is the season to do it.

♦ ...SPEAK YOUR TRUTH. Ruled by Mercury, Gemini is one of the great communicators of the zodiac, so this is the season to speak your truth and use your voice to express yourself and ask for what you want, need, and desire. This may mean some hard conversations, boundary setting, and moving out of your comfort zone, but the results will be so worth it. Remember to speak from your heart in a loving way that's true to you.

End-of-spring Moons

The end-of-spring season brings us the Gemini new moon and Sagittarius full moon.

THE GEMINI NEW MOON

The Gemini new moon enables you to connect the dots, see what you did not see before, and realize how you are being called to do things differently. You may find yourself in your head a lot over this moon, as she helps you to see where you hold yourself back and stay stuck in the same stories, narratives, doubts, and fears.

This moon will show you how you stay in your comfort zone, and all that is possible for you if you break free and expand. And if you're ready, it will give you the courage to finally see the truth and all the tools you need to be able to move forwards, start anew, and make a change.

Mini new-moon ritual
Journal on what could be possible for you if you broke beyond all your doubts, fears, expectations, and stories. If you knew without question that everything would work out, what changes would you make? Let this be your guide and start to make those changes now.

THE SAGITTARIUS FULL MOON
Under this freedom-seeking full moon, you'll be able to see where you limit yourself and keep yourself stuck and small; you'll feel literally claustrophobic in the parts of your life that don't allow you your full expression, potential and personal freedom.

This is a full moon that wants you to seek the meaning of your life, make life choices that empower you and experience the world —and life—in a whole new way.

Under this full moon, it's time to free yourself from all that restricts you and move into a whole new part of your life adventure.

Mini full-moon ritual
Hold a releasing ritual around any parts of you or your life that feel like they bind you; this could also include any scared parts of you or ones that doubt what you're capable of, as well as old stories and beliefs. Say goodbye to these things, maybe writing a letter to these parts of yourself or your life (you can burn it afterward),

letting them know what you have learned from them but saying it's time to let them go.

How to Connect with Nature and Her Wisdom

Look out for baby birds learning to fly so that they can leave the nest. I always take such inspiration from this journey they go on, as they simply don't give up. The first few times a bird tries to fly, the chances are they will end up falling. But rather than see this as failure, they try again and again, until one day it happens. A bird will also never learn to fly until it leaves the comfort zone of its nest. We can all learn so much from this.

"Stop and smell the roses" is a rephrasing of a similar senti-ment written by the golfer Walter Hagen in 1956: "Don't hurry. Don't worry. And be sure to smell the flowers along the way"—

Sacred Season Made Simple

Nature is inspiring you to take a last growth spurt toward what you want for yourself and your life.

Reflect on changes you need to make to grow into your full potential, and where and how you are holding yourself back.

Use the change-loving energies of Gemini to make relevant adjustments in your life to take you closer toward where you want to go.

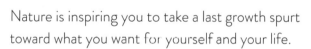

99

the overriding message being that we should stop and appreciate the beauty of life as we go through it. This season gives us the perfect opportunity to do just this, as many varieties of roses are at their best. Summer is also fast approaching, and this prompts us to pause and enjoy what is in front of us.

As the season turns, roses are also a powerful reminder of change, endings and beginnings, as they go through their continual cycles of bud, bloom, and dormancy. You must deadhead a rose to encourage further blooms, showing us that we sometimes need to let go of what's old to welcome in the new.

A moment of reflection

What have you learned about this season, and how can you apply it to your own life? How are you being called to make changes and push beyond your comfort zone? What can you do to start to live the life that you want?

Reflect on the last season; did you do what you committed to doing?

This season I commit to:

_____

_____

_____

THE SACRED SEASON OF

Summer

START-OF-SUMMER SEASON: 21 June–22 July—the sacred season for opportunities (pp. 103–116)

MID-SUMMER SEASON: 23 July–22 August—the sacred season for abundance (pp. 117–130)

END-OF-SUMMER SEASON: 23 August–21 September—the sacred season for getting back on track 1 (pp. 131–140)

CHAPTER 9

Start-of-summer Season—the Sacred Season for Opportunities

DATES: 21 June–22 July

WHEEL-OF-THE-YEAR CELEBRATION: summer solstice, approximately 21 June

ZODIAC SEASON: Cancer

MOONS THIS SEASON: Cancer new moon and Capricorn full moon

REFLECT THIS SEASON ON: embracing summer and all the opportunities it offers, and saying yes to life.

LOOK OUT IN NATURE FOR: the chorus of insects, full meadows brimming with life, and haymaking.

The start of summer brings us the summer solstice, Cancer season and the season when the earth and Nature are at their peak, filled with energy and life.

With the long days of warm, bright sunshine, activating the growth in everything around us, Nature is in full manifestation and creation mode. It feels like opportunity is everywhere, and Nature is showing us that anything is possible. Take inspiration from her, with everything in full bloom, to grow your desires and ideas, and expand beyond any limitations. This is the season to grow into all that you can be.

Even though this month heralds the start of warmer, sunnier days, we get the longest day and shortest night of the year this season. From here, the days will shorten, and we start to return toward the dark cycle of the year. This is the perfect reminder that nothing lasts forever, and that we should enjoy and embrace summer and all that it offers as much as we can, while we can.

This is the season to celebrate being alive and to use this outward expansive energy of summer to move out there into the light; let yourself shine and be seen, and make the most of every opportunity that comes your way.

A sacred pause

As we enter the second half of the traditional year, this is the ideal time to pause and check in with where you are at this midpoint. Acknowledge how far you have come and what you have achieved, any lessons learned, and all the blessings the first half of the year has already brought you.

Be honest about whether you are still aligned with your goals for the year. Reinvigorate them if you need to and decide what you want the second half of this year to bring.

Consider how you can enjoy and live life to the full over the next few months, saying yes to all the opportunities that summer offers.

JOURNAL PROMPTS FOR THE SACRED PAUSE

♦ What have you achieved so far this year?

♦ What did you think you wanted at the start of this year that may no longer be true for you? What do you want instead?

♦ What are you ready to say yes to over summer?

Start-of-summer Altar

Add oranges, yellows, reds, or gold to your altar to honor the power and life-giving energy of the sun.

Decorate your altar with greenery, particularly oak leaves, and midsummer blooms, especially wildflowers. Add a candle or sun-catcher to represent the sun's light.

Add symbols of all that you want to experience over summer— maybe images of places you'd like to visit or adventures you'd like to go on and things you would like to welcome into your life.

Start-of-summer Daily Rituals

Embrace these daily rituals to help you connect to the essence of this season and Nature's guidance.

SAY YES

At the beginning of each day, simply say "yes" to yourself a few times. Yes to a new day, yes to opportunities coming your way, yes to your dreams coming true, yes to life. Just say yes.

TAP INTO YOUR INTUITION

Your intuition is always there, waiting to guide you to wonderful new opportunities. It is a felt sense, rather than a thought—so practice tuning into the wisdom of your body daily and how things "feel." When you need to make a decision, "feel" it in your body: how would it feel in your body to say yes? How would it feel in your body to say no? It will be subtle at first, but the more you work with and act on your intuition, the more you'll learn to trust it.

MANIFESTING CRYSTAL MAGIC

Set your summer intentions on a citrine crystal to help you to activate and magnetize your dreams toward you. Make a list of those intentions and of what you want to manifest into your life over this season, then hold your citrine and whisper it all to your crystal. Ask it to help you draw toward you all you need to make this dream come true and bring you the inner power, light, and courage to go after your dreams.

Keep your citrine on your altar with your list underneath it and, once a day, hold/meditate with your crystal, visualizing that all your dreams have come true and how that feels. Be open to receiving intuitive insights and signs that take you closer to your dreams.

Crystals for the Start of Summer

- ◆ CITRINE As the crystal of abundance and manifestation, this is the perfect one to have on hand through this season to help attract new opportunities and bring to life all that you desire.

- ◆ MOONSTONE Strongly connected to feminine energy and intuition, moonstone will help you to get beneath the noise of your mind and the outside world, and into your deeper wisdom and inner intuitive knowing.

Affirmations for the Start of Summer

- ◆ "I am open to new opportunities."

- ◆ "I listen to my heart."

- ◆ "I say yes to life."

Ways to Work with Cancer Season

After Gemini season brought us change and an influx of insight, information, and inspiration, Cancer season now wants you to take what you've learned through the year so far and integrate it into your being, so that it becomes knowing.

Cancer season takes us into the second half of the traditional year and brings a chance to review the first half, so that we may move on with a deeper knowing of who we are and what we want.

It's so easy in our modern-day world to get pulled way off track, especially when the busyness of summer kicks in. Use Cancer season to find your way back to who you are, what you want, and what is important to you. Cancer season encourages rest, reconnection, nurturing and focusing of precious energy on what and who matter most to you. Let your emotions and intuition be your guide to what you say yes or no to. The summer is only just getting started and you don't want to burn yourself out too quickly.

Unafraid of deep emotions, Cancer season will help you to uncover, process, heal, and release any emotional baggage, so you don't need to carry it with you into the second half of the year.

Rather than get lost in your emotions, allow them to inspire and point you in the direction of those areas in your life that need to change. Deeply intuitive, Cancer season will help you to get in touch with the inner world of your dreams and intuition, so that you may tune into your heart and soul, and they can guide you into the second half of the year and all that awaits you.

USE CANCER SEASON TO...

♦ ...RECONNECT WITH YOURSELF. Especially if you've already found yourself being pulled in a million different directions, use this next month to really come home to and embrace yourself. Prioritize more self-care, self-reflection, and self-awareness, particularly if you're sensing a mid-year burnout on the horizon.

♦ ...PRACTICE DEEP HEALING AND FORGIVENESS. As one of the most emotional signs of the zodiac, this is the perfect season for healing and forgiveness of anything you don't want to carry through the rest of the year. Write out a list of any emotions, resentments, hurts, and pains you've been carrying around and begin the healing process this month.

♦ ...GO INWARDS AND LISTEN TO YOUR SOUL. Your intuition will be strong as the sun moves through Cancer, so this could be the perfect time to develop a daily meditation practice to listen to the whispers of your soul and keep you anchored within yourself and what you want as summer starts to speed up.

Start-of-summer Moons

The start-of-summer season brings us the Cancer new moon and Capricorn full moon.

THE CANCER NEW MOON

The moon in her home sign of Cancer pulls our awareness inwards into our private inner worlds, our deepest hopes and dreams, the parts of ourselves that we keep hidden away, and our inner yearnings that we are aware of, but others aren't.

As is often the way with the moon in Cancer, you may find yourself deep in your emotions, feeling all the feelings. Just as the moon embraces her ebb and flow—and this is where much of her power comes from—she wants you to tap into the power of your emotional world.

Our emotions are messengers, signposts—they hold such powerful insight and information for us and, as such, they should be honored and accepted rather than suppressed and denied.

This new moon wants you to create a safe space within, for you to know your inner world and trust yourself, your intuition, what you are being shown, what you know and what is stirring within you, calling for attention.

Mini new-moon ritual

Take a mini retreat under this moon, even if it's just an evening alone to be with yourself, and take an honest look at your life. Sit with your emotions; they are bringing you the awareness of something. Journal on how you're feeling and what your emotions are calling your attention to—what they are showing you about what is out of alignment in your life and what you need to be aware of in this moment.

THE CAPRICORN FULL MOON

Although Capricorn is an earthy grounding sign, the days around a Capricorn moon can very often feel unsettled and unsteady, shaking the foundations of your life to see what is real and lasting, helping you to release what you've been clinging to.

The first full moon after the summer solstice, this one comes along to help you wrap up the old, so that you can enter the new, finally leaving behind anything you don't want to take forwards, removing any self-imposed limitations, letting go of fears and illuminating the way, showing you how to plan ahead, so that nothing can prevent you from reaching your goals.

Mini full-moon ritual

Under this full moon, ask the deeper—perhaps more difficult—questions about your life: what have you been holding on to, even though you've known for a while it isn't working? What needs reshuffling, restructuring, or removing from your life?

How to Connect with Nature and Her Wisdom

With the lengthening days, get outside as often as you can. Walk among Nature and feel the fullness, abundance, and manifestation in the air all around you. The trees are tall and lush, the meadows are bursting with life and wildlife is busy and buzzing around. Let Nature show you how to make the most of life—and say yes.

For me, there is nothing more nostalgic than strawberry picking, and nothing tastes better than sweet, ripe strawberries you've picked yourself! The strawberry has long been considered the fruit of love, with associations with Venus. But perhaps most interesting is that they are not officially a berry and the little seeds on the outside are the actual fruit, each one containing a single seed inside it. Strawberries are literally filled with opportunities for growth!

Spend time with sunflowers—the embodiment of summer. Rows of tall yellow heads face the sun, bringing joy and happiness to all who lay eyes on them. Like the sunflowers, turn your face to the sun and look for the light in every situation.

The Summer Solstice

♦ **DATE CELEBRATED:** approximately 21 June

♦ **ALSO KNOWN AS:** Litha or Midsummer

The summer solstice held deep significance for our ancestors, as marked by the many monuments around the world that align to it, such as Stonehenge and the Temple of the Sun in Machu Picchu (see p. 22).

Our ancestors relied on what grew in Nature for survival, so seeing her in full growth must have been cause for celebration. Bonfires were lit on the summer solstice to represent the power of the sun and guarantee a good harvest. Cattle were driven through the smoke and people jumped the fire to welcome abundance, the height of the year's crops being predicted by the highest jump. The ashes of the fire were then spread on the fields to ensure a good harvest. There was dancing, singing, merriment, and feasting to rejoice the sun at the peak of its power, and everyone stayed up all night to watch the sunrise and celebrate the longest day of the year.

The Oak King was celebrated for being at the height of his power and strength, granting fertility and abundance to the land, crops, and people (before losing in battle to the Holly King who takes over and rules over the winter solstice).

SPEND THE SUMMER SOLSTICE WITH YOUR SOUL

The summer solstice is the longest day and shortest night of the year. It is the doorway to the second half of the year and a time for reflection, completion, and celebration.

As mentioned earlier (see p. 20), the word "solstice" literally means stopping or standing still, making it the ideal time to be still and check in with where you are. Most of all, as you stand on this threshold to the second half of the year, it's time to truly decide who you want to be and what you want to make of the next six months. It's all up to you.

On this day of full solar power, it's a time to celebrate yourself, life and abundance. It's a day to use the peak of the strength and power of the sun to add light and energy and life to all you wish to be and have in your life.

It is especially powerful to watch the sunrise on the summer solstice to witness the beginning of the longest day of the year and welcome the light and power of the sun into your life.

SUMMER-SOLSTICE RITUALS

Set time aside in the days around the summer solstice to dedicate to these ritual practices and make the most of this seasonal transition.

Make a love to-do list

This time of year is all about celebrating summer, joy and happiness, so make a love to-do list, filled with all the things you would love to do over the coming months. Mark out time in your diary for these things and make some exciting plans to simply bring more fun, freedom, and laughter into your life.

Review, release, and renew

Look back on the year so far and celebrate what you achieved, what you learned, and how you grew. Then decide what you need to leave behind, so that you can fully step into and embrace the second half of the year. Reflect on who you want to be over the next six months and how you're being called to step forwards and shine.

Visit an oak tree

The oak, known as the king of the forest, has long been the center of solstice celebrations, when the Oak King was worshipped. The Celtic word for oak is "duir," meaning doorway, taking us into the second half of the year. It is also thought that the word druid originated from this and meant knower of the oak tree.

Meditate with these mighty beings representing strength, knowledge, and wisdom, and ask for answers and guidance on anything you are bringing to life over the summer.

Remember that an acorn has within it everything it needs to become a mighty oak. And the same applies to you. When you were born, you had everything already within you to be able to grow into and become something magnificent. Be inspired by how the acorn becomes an oak and believe in all that you are capable of.

SUMMER-SOLSTICE JOURNAL PROMPTS

♦ What have you achieved so far this year?

♦ As you stand on the threshold to the second part of the year, what is no longer coming through that doorway with you?

♦ What do you want for you and your life in the last half of this year?

♦ How are you going to wholeheartedly follow these dreams and bring them to life? What do you need to do?

♦ How are you being called to step into your full power and shine?

♦ Finish this sentence: As I step into the second half of this year, I will allow my inner light to shine by...

Sacred Season Made Simple

Nature is inspiring you to grow, expand, create, and follow new opportunities—anything feels possible.

Acknowledge how far you have come at this halfway point of the traditional year and celebrate what you have achieved.

Let Cancer season show you how to use your emotions as signposts and trust your intuition.

The summer solstice will help you to move into the next six months and shine, deciding who you want to be and what you want the second half of the year to bring.

A moment of reflection

What have you learned about this season, and how can you apply it to your own life? How are you being called to grow, follow your intuition, and expand beyond limitations? What can you do to make changes in this second half of the year and what can you say yes to?

Reflect on the last season; did you do what you committed to doing?

This season I commit to:

_____

_____

_____

_____

CHAPTER 10

Mid-summer Season —the Sacred Season for Abundance

DATES: 23 July–22 August

WHEEL-OF-THE-YEAR CELEBRATION: Lammas, 1 August

ZODIAC SEASON: Leo

MOONS THIS SEASON: Leo new moon and Aquarius full moon

REFLECT THIS SEASON ON: what you are most grateful for in your life, how you've changed and grown, and on celebrating life.

LOOK OUT IN NATURE FOR: the first signs of the leaves turning, fruits and berries appearing, and heather emerging.

Mid-summer brings us Leo season and Lammas, the cross-quarter festival that represents the peak of summer and the abundance that fills Nature and our lives, as we begin to gather in the first harvest of the year.

Nature has moved from growth to ripening and is now giving generously of her gifts for all to enjoy. This is the time for you and Nature to appreciate all that you have grown, brought to life, and manifested over the last few months.

Everywhere we look, Nature is overflowing with abundance, life, and beauty, and wants us too to celebrate the fullness of our lives and all that we have.

This is the season to live life to the full, gather in and enjoy all that you have been working toward and celebrate everything that summer is bringing your way. It is a season of wild abandon, for trusting and believing, just like Nature, that your every desire will be met, and life will give you all that you need.

It might have felt like summer could last forever, but we are now at the peak of its energies, and the very first signs of autumn are starting to show, letting us know that we need to prepare for a transition in seasons. So this is a last push to bring anything else you want to life, so that you can harvest it at the autumn equinox, and to make the most of and fully enjoy what is left of summer.

A sacred pause

One thing we don't do enough of as humans is celebrate ourselves and our achievements. So as this season turns, take a sacred pause to do just that.

Celebrate what you have achieved, where in your life you are reaping what you have sown, what you have manifested into your life, and what is finally coming to life and fruition. Celebrate that you did it.

JOURNAL PROMPTS FOR THE SACRED PAUSE

♦ What are you celebrating now?

♦ What has been your greatest achievement this year— and in your life—so far?

♦ Celebrate you: list what you are good at, what you most love about yourself, and what you offer and bring to the world just by being you.

Mid-summer Altar

Mix the greens of summer with the light browns, yellows, and golds of the coming autumn.

Add sunflowers or any bright and beautiful fresh flowers, heather, meadowsweet, or bunches of crops—or even a corn doll, if you can find or make one.

Place items on your altar that represent something you've achieved so far this year that you're proud of, as a reminder of what is possible for you. You may also place your list of why you should be celebrated on your altar to remind yourself daily of how wonderful you are.

Mid-summer Daily Rituals

Embrace these daily rituals to help you connect to the essence of this season and Nature's guidance.

OPEN UP TO ABUNDANCE

Each morning, as soon as you get out of bed, open your heart and arms wide and say out loud, "I am open to all the love, luck, and abundance in the world."

Notice all the abundance you receive every day and welcome that in, saying "thank you." When someone gives you something, thank them and receive it with gratitude—whether it's a gift or a compliment, or someone lets you out in traffic or buys you a coffee, or simply a smile from a stranger. Whatever it is, simply say "thank you."

ACTIVATE YOUR INNER SUNSHINE

The manipura (or solar plexus) chakra is like our own personal inner sunshine. Situated just beneath the rib cage, above the belly button, this is the center of energy, will, and achievement, and is where all our power to manifest comes from.

Bring your palms together and rub them vigorously, until you feel some heat. Then, closing your eyes, take your hands about shoulder-distance apart, palms facing each other. Begin to slowly bring your palms together; at some point, you will begin to feel a little bit of resistance. Start to gently bounce your palms around this ball of energy, feeling it take shape between your hands. You may wish to fill this glowing energy ball with your intentions and desires. When you are ready, place it into the manipura chakra, feeling this bright, radiant sun at your center being filled with even more light and energy, and glowing even brighter. Feel as if you are now magnetic to all your intentions, manifesting them easily toward you.

CELEBRATE LIFE

Find something to celebrate each day. Whenever something good happens, celebrate it. And don't forget to celebrate *you*. Look in the mirror at the end of each day and tell yourself what you did well today and what you are proud of yourself for.

Crystals for Mid-summer

♦ SUNSTONE If you want to shine this season—and in life—look no further than sunstone. Harnessing the power of the sun, it will bring positive energy, power, and light into your life.

♦ PYRITE A crystal of wealth and abundance, pyrite will help attract to you all that you desire. Its name means fire and, true to its name, pyrite will encourage willpower and confidence and ignite a fire in your soul.

Affirmations for Mid-summer

♦ "Thank you for the abundance that fills my life."

♦ "I deserve all that life has to offer."

♦ "I celebrate life."

Ways to Work with Leo Season

Taking what you learned about yourself in the emotional depths of Cancer season, Leo season comes along to help you proudly radiate out your most authentic, true, and powerful self into the world.

Ruled by the sun and ruler of the heart, Leo wants you to shine bright and light up the world in the way that only you can. Leo shows you that there is no one else in the world like you, and that the world needs you.

Leo wants you to find freedom in self-expression and creativity, and to liberate yourself from any captivity in your life. This season will help you to feel limitless—as though anything is possible. Use Leo's and the sun's energy to make yourself magnetic to all that you desire and to shine your authentic light into the world.

Just like the sun, Leo season brings light, joy, play, and warmth into our lives and inspires us all to shine. Leo shows us that life is an adventure and, most of all, that it should be fun.

Use this season to step up and become the leader of your life. Be brave, be courageous, be bold, and fearlessly go after what you want. Seek joy, happiness, and fun. Fall in love with yourself, with life, with love.

USE LEO SEASON TO...

♦   ...LIVE FROM YOUR HEART. Leo rules the heart, and so this is the season to heal, open, and live from your heart and follow it to where it leads you. Place your hands over your heart daily and check in with how it feels; ask what it needs today and listen to what your heart wants to tell you.

♦   ...BE BOLD AND BRAVE AND BELIEVE IN YOURSELF. Leo season teaches you that it's safe to be all of you and take up space. So take a risk this season, go after what you want, and don't be afraid to shine—the world needs your light.

♦   ...BE MORE PLAYFUL. Leo season brings a childlike quality, so have more fun now. Mark out time in your diary to do things that simply bring you joy; try something different, take a spontaneous adventure, make memories, and laugh as much as you can. Let loose and squeeze every last bit of fun out of summer.

Mid-summer Moons

The mid-summer season brings us the Leo new moon and Aquarius full moon.

THE LEO NEW MOON

The Leo new moon is here to help you shine brightly as your most powerful, authentic, and aligned self, knowing that you are worth more and have more to offer.

This is a new moon to set big intentions from your heart and soul, go after your dreams, and contribute to the world in the way that only you can.

Mini new-moon ritual

No one else can do what you do in the way that you do it, so take some time under this moon to imagine what the world needs that only you can offer.

What are you being called to manifest, create, and initiate? The dreams within you are there for a reason—because only you can make them come true. Write down all that you can offer, all the dreams that are alive within you, and ways you can allow yourself to shine your light out into the world. Then go out there and do it.

THE AQUARIUS FULL MOON

This full moon is here to help you embrace all of who you are—your individuality, your truth, and what makes you authentically you. When you fully embrace who you are, you move through life differently, no longer as affected by things outside of you.

This full moon wants you to break out of expectations—the need to be accepted and understood, for approval and validation or permission from anyone else. Let people meet, see, and know the true you, so that you are then accepted simply for who and what you are.

Aquarius energy teaches us that true freedom and liberation begin with us. As we give ourselves the freedom to be ourselves and live our truth and follow our hearts, we give everyone around us permission and motivation to do the same.

Mini full-moon ritual

Realize that all change starts with you. If you feel like your life is on hold, where are you putting things on hold? If you feel power-less, where in your life do you give away your power? If you feel restricted, where do you put restrictions on yourself and what is possible for you? If you don't feel free, where do you not allow yourself the freedom to be who you are? Journal on what changes you need to make.

How to Connect with Nature and Her Wisdom

During these long, lazy last days of summer, spend as much time as you can in Nature. Lie in lush green grass, sit against a tree in full bloom, or wander alongside hedgerows brimming with berries; feel the abundance that is present all around you. See how Nature has everything she needs and gives freely of all that she has.

Look out for bales of hay appearing in the fields as a reminder that there is a perfect time for everything. Finding the right time to harvest over the next few weeks is crucial in haymaking to ensure the correct stage of plant growth and nutritional value. A beautiful prompt to us not to rush, but not to wait too long either before going after what we want! Traditionally, this would have been one of the hardest and busiest times for our ancestors, as the whole community joined in the haymaking, so in their honor, balance out some of your hard work with lots of play.

This season heather begins to light up the moorland, trans-forming everything into a sea of pink and purple, teaching us how to truly stand out and be seen. Heather grows in hostile terrain and under extreme conditions, showing us how something beautiful can often come out of the hardest times.

Lammas

- ◆ **DATE CELEBRATED:** 1 August

- ◆ **ALSO KNOWN AS:** Lughnasadh

As far back as the neolithic era, this was the beginning of the time of harvest, when the first grain was cut and celebrated. The name Lammas comes from the term "loaf mass," as the first loaves of bread of the season were baked from the fresh crop and shared among the community. Gratitude was given and offerings made for the gifts of the earth, and here the hard work started of gathering in the crops to provide stores for the coming winter.

Whereas the first sheaf that was cut was baked into the bread, the last was made into a corn doll, which was decorated with ribbons and paraded through the village. It was kept as a good-luck talisman, before being plowed back into the earth the following Imbolc (see p. 205) to ensure a good crop the next year.

Once the crops were gathered, the celebrations began, with the usual feasting, drinking, dancing, and honoring of the harvest and how it would get the village through the upcoming winter.

This was a celebration associated with the Celtic sun god, Lugh, who gave his power to the crop to grow and then sacrificed his life with the cutting of the grain, so that the community would survive. The sun's power now begins to wane.

In folklore, John Barleycorn (a fictional character who represented the crop of barley harvested each autumn) was also celebrated and honored. Seen as the spirit of the crops, and mostly associated with the drinks made from them (such as beer and whisky), each year John Barleycorn had to surrender his life, so the community would be sustained, but he lived on in the drinks that were enjoyed over the autumn and winter seasons.

SPEND LAMMAS WITH YOUR SOUL

Lammas is the cross-quarter festival that represents the peak of summer and the first gathering of our inner harvest, as hints of autumn begin to show. It's the halfway point between the summer solstice and autumn equinox, when Nature is at the peak of abundance, growth, and expansion, ripe and ready to be harvested.

It's the time when we too will begin to see the fruits of what we have been working toward, as we reap the rewards and celebrate the joys of summer and the abundance in our lives and all around us.

We also begin to turn our attention from the outside world and what we have manifested and grown out there, to our inner worlds. As we move toward autumn, our energy and awareness will be pulled inwards, and it's here, at Lammas, that we gather and ensure we have all we need within us to sustain us over the autumn and winter hibernation.

Today is a day for connecting with our inner abundance and bounty, giving thanks for what we have manifested, grown, and welcomed into our lives.

LAMMAS RITUALS

Set time aside in the days around Lammas to dedicate to these ritual practices and make the most of this seasonal transition.

Gather your inner harvest

Write out a gratitude list for all that you are most grateful for in your life right now. List the areas in which you are feeling richest —friends, relationships, work, your home—and celebrate the abundance that fills your life.

Look at what you have achieved and manifested into your life over the last few months. Recognize where in your life you are reaping what you have sown and celebrate it being here now.

Review your intentions

Look back on your spring-equinox intentions, what you wanted to grow in your life over spring and what hasn't yet manifested in your life. Get honest about whether these were things you truly wanted and if, perhaps, it's now time to let them go, or whether you need to give them some more time, love, and attention over this last part of summer to help them come to life.

Reflect on your own growth

Take stock of your inner harvest and what flourished within you over spring and summer by reflecting on how much you have grown and changed this year. Look at any challenges you faced, how you overcame them, and what you are most proud of yourself for. Look at where you trusted, supported, and believed in yourself and anything you might have done differently, so that you can learn from that and grow in the future.

LAMMAS JOURNAL PROMPTS

♦ What has been your biggest lesson over summer?

♦ Where have you grown most over the summer?

♦ What has not manifested in your life? Did you truly want it? Does it need to be reconsidered, reflected on, adapted, or let go of altogether, as you move into autumn?

♦ How is your energy at this peak busyness of summer? Are you feeling exhausted or burned out? Is there an inner nudge, urging you to begin to slow down? How can you start to honor this over the coming weeks?

◆ Looking ahead toward the autumn equinox in September, what do you need to give some more time, love, and attention to now, so that you can harvest it and welcome it in the autumn?

◆ As you start to turn from outer growth and what you have brought into your life in the outside world to inner growth, what are you going to nurture in your inner world? What do you want to bring to life within yourself? More self-love? Self-care? Self-belief? Kindness? What inner seeds are you planting?

Sacred Season Made Simple

Nature is inspiring you to appreciate and enjoy life and what is left of summer.

Reflect on what you have to celebrate in life.

Use the bold, bright energies of Leo to allow yourself to shine.

Lammas will help you to gather your inner harvest and feel the abundance that fills your life.

A moment of reflection

What have you learned about this season, and how can you apply it to your own life? How are you being called to celebrate and open up to receiving more abundance in your life? What can you do to be bold and brave and make the best of the end of summer?

Reflect on the last season; did you do what you committed to doing?

This season I commit to:

_____

_____

_____

_____

CHAPTER 11

End-of-summer Season —the Sacred Season for Getting Back on Track

DATES: 23 August–21 September

WHEEL-OF-THE-YEAR CELEBRATION: none

ZODIAC SEASON: Virgo

MOONS THIS SEASON: Virgo new moon and Pisces full moon

REFLECT THIS SEASON ON: what you need to complete, getting your life back on track and planting seeds for the future.

LOOK OUT IN NATURE FOR: the first signs of autumn—acorns, horse chestnuts, and seeds falling to the earth and hedgerows bursting with berries.

The end of summer brings us Virgo season to help wrap up summer and transition into a shift in season.

The sun begins to wane to a warm golden light at this time of year, and we see the first shades of gold in the trees, as autumn beckons and Nature starts to go to ground. The summer blooms have given way to seed heads, which will begin to drop over the coming weeks and remain in the earth over winter, until they burst into life again next spring. The crop fields have been cut, leaving stubble behind, and vegetation is dying back; yet we also see seeds and nuts ripening and the hedgerows are heavy with berries.

There is a contrasting energy in Nature at this time of year and we may feel the same: not quite ready for summer to be over but recognizing that it's time to knuckle down again and get back on track with our lives.

Nature can look a little messy over this season, as she prepares her last harvest for autumn, and we are asked to do the same. This is the time to look at what in our lives feels untidy, having abandoned certain things over the height of summer. It's the time to do what's needed to make the most of the last part of the year.

And just as Nature is dropping her seeds to ensure future growth, we need to start looking ahead at what we can do now, so that we may grow and create in the future.

Nature is winding down summer, and she is asking us to do the same: to consider what we need to finish up and where we need to begin to draw our energy inwards and gather what we need to sustain us through the darker months ahead.

A sacred pause

For many people, this season brings a back-to-school kind of feeling, so take a sacred pause here to feel where you need to get back on track. Look at what got left behind in the wild abandon of summer and where you left things unfinished (or not even started), what needs wrapping up, finishing up, or what you need to be getting on with now.

This season sets a lot of the groundwork for what will sustain you through autumn and winter, and what will grow in your life again come next spring. Look too at any last big push you can give now to achieve what you wanted this year and to end the year on a high.

JOURNAL PROMPTS FOR THE SACRED PAUSE

♦ Where did you go off track over summer?

♦ What do you need to wrap up, complete, and finish this season?

♦ What do you need to start now to finish the year on a high and prepare for future growth?

End-of-summer Altar

Green, yellow, and brown are the colors of this season. Perhaps gather some green and golden leaves for your altar to represent the beauty of this time of transition between summer and autumn.

Gather seeds, acorns, and horse chestnuts as a reminder of what you want to germinate over the autumn and winter, so that it can grow in your life in the future. Add visual representations and symbols of what you are growing in your life longer term. Add reminders, too, of what you want to wrap up, finish, and complete—maybe even a to-do list that you can check in with daily to get you back on track.

End-of-summer Daily Rituals

Embrace these daily rituals to help you connect to the essence of this season and Nature's guidance.

FIND A RITUAL AND ROUTINE

Find a daily ritual and routine that you can stick to this whole season to bring you back into alignment with yourself and your life after summer. This could be meditation, exercise, journaling, or anything that nurtures you at this point. Pick a time of day and decide how long you can commit to this daily—and make sure that you do it.

In the same way, create a bedtime ritual. Often, we stay up much later in summer, but now is the time to begin to turn toward getting more rest again. Set a bedtime, prepare for it through winding down, meditation, and conscious quiet time. Carve out this time for you as a non-negotiable every day and you'll see such a huge difference in your life after only a few weeks.

PRIORITIZE PASSION PROJECTS

Spend some time each day on a passion project, hobby, or something that brings you joy. This is important not only for general wellbeing, but also to see how your side hustle could grow into a full-time dream in the future. Perhaps invest in a course that you can dedicate some time to every day to take you closer to what you want.

LOOK TO THE LONGER TERM

As the light begins to fade, and it becomes clear that the darker months are coming, look ahead to what you are growing in your life longer term. Let your future dreams be the fuel that keeps you alight from within over the autumn and winter. Create a vison board under the Virgo new moon (see mini new-moon ritual, p. 138) and look at it every day, visualizing and staying connected to what you want. Do one little thing daily to take you a step closer to the future you want.

Crystals for the End of Summer

- ♦ BLACK TOURMALINE This crystal will help you to ground and come back to earth. It will support you in creating healthy new habits and help you to take care of yourself and your energy.

- ♦ AMETHYST This is a crystal that will help you to visualize what you want from your life and then set realistic goals and steps to take you there. It will support you in getting organized and planning, and encourage you to believe that you can create what you want for your future.

Affirmations for the End of Summer

♦   "My daily rituals and routines support me."

♦   "I take care of myself and my wellbeing."

♦   "Small steps take me closer to where I want to be."

Ways to Work with Virgo Season

After Leo season helped you to enjoy a summer of fun, Virgo season helps you to take care of yourself and get your life back on track.

As summer starts to wind down, Virgo brings an earthy energy to return you to reality and get things in order. Methodical and pragmatic, Virgo brings you ritual, routine, and practical next steps, helping you to complete some things, get started on others, and organize your life.

Virgo is also the healer of the zodiac, asking you to begin to take a healthier approach to life and to prioritize yourself, creating some good daily habits that will benefit you through the rest of the year and beyond.

This season will help you to settle back into a structure and give attention to those parts of your life that were forgotten in the summer months, helping you to find joy in the daily tasks and routines that give your life meaning and focus.

USE VIRGO SEASON TO...

♦   ...BE OF SERVICE. Virgo loves being of service, so give back this season and offer help and support to others wherever you can. Surprise loved ones with thoughtful gestures and do simple little daily acts of service as often as you can, like giving up your seat on public transport or letting someone out in traffic. Give from your heart with no expectation and your life will feel so much more wholesome.

♦ ... TAKE CARE OF YOUR HEALTH. Especially if you had a summer of indulgence, now is the time to look after yourself once more. Virgo encourages you to treat yourself with love and respect, and up your wellness game. Commit to an exercise routine, get more active, clean up your diet, meditate for your mind, get more quality sleep, and care for yourself as best you can.

♦ ... MAKE SMALL DAILY CHANGES. Rather than a big dramatic life overhaul, Virgo shows that it's the little day-to-day things that get the biggest results. Look at your routines and habits and make small daily changes that will not only help you to feel better in the moment but contribute to what you want longer term and where you want to go.

End-of-summer Moons

The end-of-summer season brings us the Virgo new moon and Pisces full moon.

THE VIRGO NEW MOON

This earthy new moon comes to help you organize your life and take action. With summer coming to an end, it's time to get clear and focus, make changes, and get things done. It's also time to look ahead at what you want and what you can do now to ensure that those things can come to fruition when the time is right.

This new moon will show you practical next steps and a logical plan, with all the information, knowledge, and support you need to be able to easily move forwards.

Mini new-moon ritual

Create a vision board over this new moon. This is a visual representation of your dreams, what you want to achieve and see happen in your life. It can be done through words, images, or pictures that stand for what you want. Place your vision board on your altar and spend time daily looking at it, visualizing all these things being in your life. Then use Virgo's energies to make a plan of small daily steps you can take to get you, gradually, closer to what you want.

THE PISCES FULL MOON

The last sign of the zodiac, and last full moon before we turn seasons and move into autumn, this one will help you to shed the old, release anything that does not serve you, and tie up loose ends.

Use the illumination of this full moon to look back over all that has happened since the summer solstice: the journey you have been on, the lessons and learnings, what has challenged and changed you.

Pisces calls you into trusting your inner voice of what is/isn't working in your life, and this full moon will show you where you got led astray over summer and where your life needs new direction in autumn.

Mini full-moon ritual

Hold an end-of-summer ritual as the summer comes to an end. Give gratitude for all that it has brought, reap the lessons and rewards, and look forward to how you want to do things differently in autumn. Make a commitment to effecting these changes.

How to Connect with Nature and Her Wisdom

Look at the seeds, horse chestnuts, and acorns that fall to the earth. It may look like these things are dying and falling away, but they are actually creating a new beginning. These seeds contain all that's needed to ensure future growth, and they will retreat into the earth to germinate before coming to life next spring. Nature never expects immediate results; rather, she lays the groundwork, preparing now for all that's to come—as should you.

This is the time of year to find apples and the hedgerows bursting with fresh blackberries, elderberries, rosehips, and wild raspberries. Gather in a final harvest and enjoy the last of Nature's abundance (just be mindful of leaving enough for the wildlife to feast on, as this is a valuable source of energy and nutrients to see them through).

Sacred Season Made Simple

Nature is inspiring you to wind down the summer and plant seeds for what you want to grow in the future.

Reflect on any last big push you can give to achieve what you wanted this year.

Use Virgo's organized and practical energy to get back on track in your life after summer.

A moment of reflection

What have you learned about this season, and how can you apply it to your own life? How are you being called to complete what needs completing and get started on what you have let slip? What seeds are you planting now for what you want in the future? And what can you do now to take you closer to what you want?

Reflect on the last season; did you do what you committed to doing?

This season I commit to:

_____

_____

_____

_____

THE SACRED SEASON OF

START-OF-AUTUMN SEASON: 22 September–22 October—the sacred season for gratitude (pp. 143–156)

MID-AUTUMN SEASON: 23 October–21 November—the sacred season for alchemy and transformation (pp. 157–170)

END-OF-AUTUMN SEASON: 22 November–20 December—the sacred season for journeying inwards (pp. 171–180)

CHAPTER 12

Start-of-autumn Season —the Sacred Season for Gratitude

DATES: 22 September–22 October

WHEEL-OF-THE-YEAR CELEBRATION: autumn equinox, approximately 22 September

ZODIAC SEASON: Libra

MOONS THIS SEASON: Libra new moon and Aries full moon

REFLECT THIS SEASON ON: what you are most grateful for, what you are ready to shed and let go of, and how you might start slowing down.

LOOK OUT IN NATURE FOR: the turning of the leaves, misty mornings, ripening fruits and berries, and seeds falling back to the earth.

The start of autumn brings us the autumn equinox, Libra season and the season when Nature begins to visibly transform, as summer makes way for autumn. The nights are starting to draw in, the sap is returning to its roots, and the leaves are changing color, as the lush green of summer gives way to the browns, oranges, reds, and golds of autumn.

The last harvest in Nature is waiting to be gathered in, and appreciated, and this is where we too begin to harvest all that has grown over spring and summer—not just in Nature, but in our own lives.

Nature is beginning to slow down and turn inwards in preparation for the impending winter, asking you to do the same. After the busyness of summer, you may feel a real dip in energy levels as the season shifts—a need to rest, slow down, and process what the year has brought you so far. The turn of season asks you to give thanks for everything you have achieved and all you have enjoyed, and to everyone who has helped along the way.

The leaves begin to fall from the trees and Nature sheds and lets go, inspiring us to cast off layers of ourselves and whatever is no longer in alignment or feeling balanced and harmonious in our lives. This marks the beginning of the inner/darker phase of the Wheel of the Year as both we and she are called upon to draw energy inwards to take care of and nourish ourselves, becoming quieter, still, and inwardly present.

A sacred pause

As the season once again shifts, take a sacred pause here to gather back all the parts of you that got lost and scattered in the busyness of summer. Become fully present, turn your awareness inwards, and check in with your heart and any parts of you that you ignored or left unattended when life got busy.

Though fun and happy, the summer months are also good for avoidance of anything deeper within us calling for attention, as we are often "too busy" to listen and too focused on the outside world. But now we are asked to slow down and turn our attention inwards, listening to our inner world and getting back in touch with ourselves.

This can be challenging, especially if you have been avoiding the lingering doubt within you that certain things in your life aren't working. But now, as Nature is doing and supporting you to do the same, it's time to let go.

JOURNAL PROMPTS FOR THE SACRED PAUSE

♦ Where did you lose, scatter, or abandon yourself and your needs over summer?

♦ What is your inner world trying to tell you?

♦ What emotions or intuitive voices have you been avoiding listening to and dealing with?

Start-of-autumn Altar

Add oranges, reds, and golds to your altar to represent the array of colors in Nature right now. Collect fallen autumn leaves, acorns, and horse chestnuts, as a reminder of the beauty in letting go of what is no longer needed and the new life that can come from this.

Let your altar be a place of gratitude for all you have and are most thankful for in your life at this turn of season. Add images, pictures, and symbols of what you achieved over spring and summer, the adventures you had, and what you have loved and appreciated most so far this year.

Start-of-autumn Daily Rituals

Embrace these daily rituals to help you connect to the essence of this season and Nature's guidance.

FEEL THE GRATITUDE

Each day, take a moment to pause and consider what you are most grateful for in this moment. Close your eyes and really feel the gratitude, allowing it to infuse your entire being. Place your hands over your heart and whisper "thank you" into it, over and over, for a few moments.

You may also start a gratitude journal, writing down three things you are most grateful for at the beginning or end of each day. Or try a gratitude jar—I love these: each time something wonderful happens, write it down on a piece of paper and place it in a jar. Watch your blessings as they grow over the weeks and months. And any time you feel stuck or low, read a few of these things from your jar and remind yourself how much you have to be grateful for.

DEVELOP A DAILY SPIRITUAL PRACTICE

Autumn is often described as the season of the soul, making this the perfect time to return inwards and connect back to your soul. A daily practice is so important at this time of year to support you not only through this transition, but to prepare you for the colder, darker days ahead by giving you a stable inner foundation to draw from.

Dedicate ten or fifteen minutes a day to this practice, which could be meditation, journaling, yoga, breathing, quiet time in contemplation, drawing—anything that feels nourishing to you and connects you back to yourself. There is only one rule: that you commit to it every day, no matter what. In this way, it becomes your foundation—your touchstone back to yourself.

EMBRACE SLOW LIVING

Over this season, notice how much you hurry through life, always rushing on to the next thing. Instead, can you make it a practice to take a slower approach? Move through your day more mindfully and do things with meaning and purpose. Savor your morning coffee, eat your food slowly, give yourself extra time to get to places, so you can appreciate the journey there. Get into bed early and read a book. Be less busy and embrace slow living; it may just change your life.

Crystals for the Start of Autumn

- ◆ AMETHYST Not only will this help you to slow down and be more mindful, it will also help to balance your emotions and connect more deeply to your inner world and intuition.

- ◆ SMOKY QUARTZ Smoky quartz will keep you grounded and connected through the turn of season, bringing you back to your roots. It will also help you to let go of and release what you no longer need.

Affirmations for the Start of Autumn

♦ "I trust and let go with ease."

♦ "I find peace, balance, and harmony in my life."

♦ "Thank you, thank you, thank you..." (repeated over)

Ways to Work with Libra Season

After a busy summer, Libra season comes to call you back into balance and begins the process of drawing you inwards, back home to you, your heart, your soul. Just as Nature is doing, this season calls you inwards to find more equilibrium between your inner and outer worlds.

Libra asks you to create an inner peace and harmony in preparation for the winter months ahead, bringing an understanding of what pulls you out of balance and alignment, helping you to make necessary adjustments in your life.

Libra also brings a big focus on relationships, particularly where there isn't mutual support and equal give and take, and asks you to deepen the most important relationship you'll ever have—the one with yourself.

USE LIBRA SEASON TO...

♦ ... FIND EQUILIBRIUM IN ALL AREAS OF YOUR LIFE. Look at what you have been worrying about and giving too much mental energy to, your work/home life balance, and who and what in your life seems to be pulling you off-kilter. Find ways that you can bring yourself back into inner peace and harmony.

♦ ... REVIEW YOUR RELATIONSHIPS. Are there people who leave you feeling depleted after spending time with them or relationships in which you do all the giving? This is a good time to have those important conversations and put boundaries in place to bring your relationships back into more balance.

♦ ... LOOK AT THE RELATIONSHIP YOU HAVE WITH SLOWING DOWN. This is the season when everything around us begins to slow down—but do you ever allow yourself to do so, or do you always have to be perpetually busy, equating your self-worth with how much you are getting done? How can you show yourself love and care this season by allowing time to slow down, rest, and listen to your inner world?

Start-of-autumn Moons

The start-of-autumn season brings us the Libra new moon and Aries full moon.

THE LIBRA NEW MOON

The Libra new moon will show you where you are out of balance and alignment within yourself—where you are not being true to yourself or giving too much of you away.

Look at where have you taken on too much and what needs to give, where you feel most out of balance in your life and what you need more of to feel whole and complete.

This is also a moon that asks you to look at your relationships with others, and whether they are in balance.

Mini new-moon ritual

The intentions you set at this new moon will be your guiding light through autumn and help you to remain true to you. So decide where you want to put your time, energy, focus, and love over these next few weeks. Set intentions that bring more balance, peace, and harmony into your life.

THE ARIES FULL MOON

This fiery first sign of the zodiac comes in strong to help you to take back control of your life and kick-start much-needed change, especially when it comes to areas of your life where you have been putting up with too little for too long, given away your power, or lost yourself.

As we move into the introspective part of the year, this full moon will urge you to take care of your own needs and to notice where you've been ignoring your inner desires and not doing things your own way.

Mini full-moon ritual

Turn back to yourself under this full moon. Look at where you've let your wellbeing slip, ignored your own needs, and haven't taken good enough care of yourself. Give yourself the same love, care, and attention that you would give to others and fill yourself back up.

How to Connect with Nature and Her Wisdom

Marvel at the sight of the whole world around you changing color, experience the crunch of leaves beneath your feet, and spend some time watching them fall from the trees. See how effortlessly Nature lets go. There is no doubt or struggle in leaves falling from the trees —Nature shows us the beauty in letting go.

Spiders appear in greater numbers now, and you will often witness the beautiful sight of their dew-laden webs on misty mornings. I'm always in awe of the intricacy of these webs and the hard work that goes into weaving them. Gazing at them reminds me of the interconnectedness of everything and the countless threads woven through our lives.

Look out for fantastic fungi. Damp weather creates the perfect conditions for mushrooms to grow and thrive in all their weird and wonderful forms. We can learn so much from fungi, but especially about connection and communication. There is much research now about mycelium, the root-like structure of mushrooms, extending far and wide beneath the soil, gathering nutrients, and forming a communication network for trees and plants to talk to each other and share nutrients and information.[11]

The Autumn Equinox

♦ DATE CELEBRATED: approximately 22 September

♦ ALSO KNOWN AS: Mabon

As far back as the neolithic era, this represented the turning point

---

11 https://www.oneearth.org/mapping-the-fungi-network-that-lives-beneath-the-soil/

in the year for agricultural communities, as the earth's productivity began to wane and preparations were made for winter. For our ancestors, it was a busy time of gathering in and taking stock of the final harvest, knowing how well the crops had done and whether there would be enough to sustain them through the winter.

After the hard work was done there was a celebration. Communities and families came together to give thanks for the year's harvest and all the abundance that Nature had provided. Feasting took place, as well as dancing and praying to the god/dess for the crops to last through winter. Many consider this to have been the original harvest festival or thanksgiving.

The term Mabon wasn't used for the autumn equinox until the 1970s, but its origins are thought to be in the Welsh mythological character Mabon ap Modron, whose name means great son. Legend goes that when he was three days old, he was kidnapped from his mother, Modron, the earth goddess, causing the light of the earth to hide. He was later rescued by King Arthur.

Modern-day druids celebrate Alban Elfed, which means the light of the water and is the feast of the autumn equinox, a ceremony thanking the earth for its gifts.

SPEND THE AUTUMN EQUINOX WITH YOUR SOUL

The autumn equinox marks the start of autumn, when the heat and busyness of summer are ending and you are now being called back toward the earth—grounding, stilling, and becoming inwardly present.

As Nature slows down and begins to draw inwards, she encourages you to do the same. Notice where you are being called to slow down and connect back to the world within—into your inner strength, power, wisdom, and, most of all, your intuition and inner knowing. It's time to connect back to the magic within you.

AUTUMN-EQUINOX RITUALS

Set time aside in the days around the autumn equinox to dedicate to these ritual practices and make the most of this seasonal transition.

Gather your inner harvest

Now is the time to reap what you have sown and gather your inner harvest. Make a list of everything you have in your life and all you have to be grateful for. Give thanks for all you have achieved and for everything and everyone who has helped you along the way. Review what has challenged you and what has changed you, and most of all the lessons behind it all. Look at where you were at Imbolc and the spring equinox and what you have manifested, achieved, and created in your life since then.

As you reap your inner harvest, it will give you a strong foundation to support you through the darkness and depths of winter, giving you the resilience to face the darkness not just on the outside, but also the inside.

Shed, release, and let go

Now is the time for shedding, releasing, and letting go of anything you don't want to take forwards with you. Trees actively shed their leaves at this time, as there is no use for them for now; let them inspire you to do the same.

One of the main reasons we grip and cling so tightly as humans is through fear: fear of what will happen if we let go, fear that there is nothing else out there, fear that we will no longer be safe or taken care of. But just as the trees know that holding on to something that is no longer working or bringing nutrients can cause stagnation—even damage—and prevent new life coming through, we can also be held back from fully living. Be inspired by Nature to drop what is no longer working for you, so as to allow new life to come through in spring.

Plant seeds for spring

All around us now seeds are falling to the earth to incubate in the soil, until they can germinate and grow next spring. In the same way, reflect on all you have learned and experienced over the year so far and decide what you want to plant within you to nurture and protect over winter, so that it can grow and flourish next spring.

With this in mind, imagine you have fast forwarded six months and it's now the spring equinox in March. Write down in as much detail as you can where you are, what you are doing, who you are with, and what your life is filled with—really visualize all that you want to have in your life by this time.

Next, consider what actions you need to take over autumn and winter to give all your seeds the best chance of growth. How can you nurture, take care of, and support them to bring this spring dream to fruition?

AUTUMN-EQUINOX JOURNAL PROMPTS

♦ Looking back, what are you most grateful for over the summer? What were the highlights and things you are most thankful for over the last three months?

♦ What have you discovered about yourself and life over the summer? What are three of your greatest lessons?

- Sum up your inner harvest here; what are you celebrating about the summer, about life, about you?

- What drains your nutrients? What (or who) in your life feels like it does not nourish, support, or sustain you?

- What are you finally ready to let go of and release, once and for all? Declare it.

- How can you support this transition? What strong roots, foundations, and beliefs do you need to develop in yourself?

Sacred Season Made Simple

Nature is inspiring you to begin to turn inwards, slow down, and let go of anything you no longer need.

Reflect on where you scattered and lost yourself over the summer and turn back to your inner world.

Use the balancing energies in Libra season and in Nature to find peace and harmony in yourself and your life.

The autumn equinox will help you to gather your inner harvest, give thanks for all you have, and plant seeds for spring.

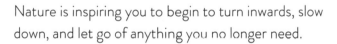

A moment of reflection

What have you learned about this season, and how can you apply it to your own life? How are you being called to slow down and turn inwards? What are you most grateful for and what do you need to shed and let go of?

Reflect on the last season; did you do what you committed to doing?

This season I commit to:

_____

_____

_____

_____

CHAPTER 13

Mid-autumn Season—the Sacred Season for Alchemy and Transformation

DATES: 23 October–21 November

WHEEL-OF-THE-YEAR CELEBRATION: Samhain, 31 October

ZODIAC SEASON: Scorpio

MOONS THIS SEASON: Scorpio new moon and Taurus full moon

REFLECT THIS SEASON ON: your inner power, magic, and intuition, and what you need to end so that something new can begin.

LOOK OUT IN NATURE FOR: the final leaves falling from the trees and covering the earth, salmon swimming upstream, and animals and Nature heading into hibernation.

Mid-autumn season brings us signs of the death/rebirth cycle, as the final leaves fall from the trees and everything in Nature seems to be dying away and retreating into the earth.

We must now accept that winter is coming and, just as Nature is doing, retreat inwards and embrace the darker and colder months ahead. Although we may feel a darkness at this time of year, in the shorter days and realization that the long days of summer are well and truly over, Nature is teaching us a beautiful lesson as she effortlessly transitions into the darkness. She allows what has been to die away, so that something brand new can be born again once the soil has regenerated and rested.

We can all learn so much from this time of year—that our best work only comes from us being rested and nurtured, and that we must let go of what has been to allow all that is yet to come.

Use the inspiration of Nature to honor the cycles of death and rebirth in your own life. Consciously make the effort to shed and release all that has ended and been completed, allowing it to gently die and fall away, so that you can create space for new opportunities and possibilities when it's time to be reborn.

Take inspiration from Nature to surrender and retreat within for rest and regeneration. Let her show you how to draw back into the shadows and turn inwards to connect to your inner world, into the stillness and the quiet, and all the mysteries and magic you contain.

A sacred pause

As the season turns and we celebrate the cycles of life, death and rebirth, take a sacred pause to reflect on what you need to say goodbye to.

This could be limiting thoughts and beliefs, people, relationships, versions of yourself, ways you've allowed yourself to be treated, or habits and behaviors that don't serve you. Reflect on how you feel about endings and whether you tend to hold on and stay stuck in the past, and what you're finally ready to let go of.

Whatever you hold on to now you will take into hibernation, so visualize being in a cave for the next few months —would you want all that you have in your current life to be in there with you?

JOURNAL PROMPTS FOR THE SACRED PAUSE

- How do you feel about endings?
- What are you finally ready to say goodbye to?
- What do you not want to take into winter hibernation with you?

Mid-autumn Altar

Orange, black, purple, and white are the colors most associated with this time of year, so fill your altar with them. Add sticks and twigs, feathers, stones and bones, and anything from the natural world that draws you.

Honor your ancestors with images of those who've gone before you and embrace your inner witch with cauldrons, pumpkins, and symbols of magic and power.

Mid-autumn Daily Rituals

Embrace these daily rituals to help you connect to the essence of this season and Nature's guidance.

WELCOME THE DARKNESS

Between now and the winter solstice is the darkest time of year. Embrace the darker mornings by doing your rituals in silence in the darkness, or by candlelight. Use the darkness and solitude to take you deeper within. We so often try to fight the darker times, both in Nature and in ourselves. But in truth, the dark gives us the opportunity to go within and explore our inner worlds, to withdraw a little from the outside world, and to take deep rest. Notice if you dread the dark winters and the prospect of being indoors more in your own company—can you instead start to see this as a chance to get to know and enjoy being with yourself?

BELIEVE IN MAGIC

Thought to be something that only exists in stories and fairy tales, I truly believe that magic is real. As Roald Dahl[12] famously said, those who don't believe in magic will never find it. So for this season, believe in it—look for it all around you, invite more of it into your everyday life, be open to miracles, and see the magic in all things.

EXPLORE YOUR INNER WISDOM

Try including oracle/tarot cards in your daily ritual practice, either asking for guidance on anything you are struggling with or pulling a card each morning as a theme for your day.

You may also want to try automatic writing. To do this, take a journal/piece of paper and a pen. Write down a question if you have one. Then close your eyes, take a few deep breaths, empty your mind, and write with no thought at all. Don't worry if the words make no sense at the beginning—just allow them to flow on to the page. If you notice yourself thinking about the words, pause, breathe, and begin again when you feel ready. This process can help you to tap into deep sources of wisdom within you and access guidance from your soul.

Crystals for Mid-autumn

♦ LABRADORITE Known as the crystal of magic and transformation, labradorite will help you to remember and awaken your own ancient inner magic.

♦ BLOODSTONE This will strengthen your intuition, give you the courage to stand strong in your power, and go inwards and feel safe in yourself.

---

12 "Those who don't believe in magic will never find it."—Roald Dahl, in *The Minpins* (2019).

Affirmations for Mid-autumn

♦ "All endings are simply new beginnings."

♦ "I embrace my inner magic."

♦ "I take back my power."

Ways to Work with Scorpio Season

Libra season helped us to find balance and harmony in our lives, and now Scorpio asks us, from this balanced place, to dive deep within for inner transformation.

If you're ready to go there, Scorpio will hold your hand and lead you on a journey of self-discovery to bring your shadows to the light, transform your hardships into your greatest lessons, and heal your deepest wounds. This intrepid sign helps you to alchemize your pain into purpose and find a true belief in your own power.

Scorpio season is going to ask you to reclaim your voice and remember your magic.

I often say that you won't leave Scorpio the same as you entered it.

USE SCORPIO SEASON TO...

♦ ...FACE YOUR SHADOWS. Put simply, your shadow is all that you deny or try to hide from in yourself. It's the parts of you that you don't like or that you don't want to claim as your own or believe about yourself; the things about you that you believe aren't acceptable or lovable. Over this season, explore how you allow your fears or shadows to hold you back and learn to embrace them and bring them to the light.

♦ …DIVE DEEP INTO YOUR INNER WORLD OF INTUITION AND KNOWING. We've been taught that intuition and inner knowing are useless, to be put aside for logical thinking. But within you lie the answers to every question and the solutions to every problem—just as everything Nature needs is within the earth and the seed. Use this season to turn inwards and access that deep knowing and intuition. Look within, rather than outside, for answers and solutions.

♦ …TAKE BACK YOUR POWER. Look at ways in which you give away your power and why. Get honest about where you seek approval, validation, and acceptance from the outside world and abandon or alter yourself to get it. And where you allow your happiness or worth to be dependent on others or things outside of you. Use this season to take back your power and become the source of your own love, validation, and approval. It's time to know your own power and worth.

Mid-autumn Moons

The mid-autumn season brings us the Scorpio new moon and Taurus full moon.

THE SCORPIO NEW MOON

This new moon is here to help you to reclaim your power and step forwards into a life of passion and purpose.

The Scorpio new moon often brings deep emotion as she uncovers what's hiding beneath the surface and asks you what you are willing to finally let go of to be who you are meant to be and have all you deserve to have.

It's going to mean dropping blame and the stories you tell yourself —like "I can't do this" or "this always happens to me" or "I can never achieve anything"—and no longer being able to hide behind your doubts, fears, and shadows. You're going to have to say what you mean and mean what you say, change your beliefs, and rise in your power, showing up fully and authentically as you.

Mini new-moon ritual

Looking back over this year, what challenges have you faced and overcome and how have you grown through them? This new moon will help you to see how your fears can become your superpower, your shame your biggest teacher and the past a doorway into your future. Look at what all these things have taught you and transform them into magic to use going forwards.

THE TAURUS FULL MOON

The Taurus full moon brings a wake-up call, dragging what has been hidden into the light. She asks us to dig deep into fears, emotions, shame, pain, and heartbreak, converting them into self-love and acceptance, and belief in your own power and magic.

As the Taurus full moon is about safety, security, and comfort, this moon is going to clearly show you where you have been holding on to a *false* sense of these things in your life and where you have stayed in your comfort zone and played it safe. She will also show where you allow your shadows to play out unconsciously and let fear, stuck emotions, and the past always hold you back.

Mini full-moon ritual

Before you head into deep hibernation, this full moon wants you to let go of old emotions that you no longer need—such as blame, resentment, shame, and anything that has been holding you down or keeping you stuck this year. As full moons also shine a light upon what isn't working in our lives, this is the perfect time to decide on what you don't want to take into hibernation with you. What has served its purpose? What can you leave behind? These things will only fester and harden even more over winter.

How to Connect with Nature and Her Wisdom

Spend time in Nature observing the phase of death, as all around is bare, brown, and seemingly dead. See how Nature honors this cycle of allowing what is old to die away, going inwards to rest and regather and, in doing so, transforms, ready for rebirth. Nature is moving into a deep meditative state; let her teach you how to go inwards, too, and be still and gather the wisdom within.

If you want to honor a loved one, did you know that you can plant a tree in their memory? This is a beautiful way to keep their memory alive while helping Nature to thrive. Search for local trusts near you to help with this, so that you have somewhere to visit over the years where you can feel your loved one living on through the lives of the trees.

How about pumpkin picking? Not only does this make a fun day out, but you get to honor the roots of Samhain (see below). And enjoy pumpkin soup! Our ancestors used turnips before Samhain traditions were taken to America and pumpkins were used instead. They would carve out scary faces and place a candle inside to ward off evil spirits. There is also the legend of Stingy Jack, who tricked the devil and ended up roaming the earth with a burning coal in a carved-out turnip (hence the term jack-o'-lantern).

Samhain

♦ DATE CELEBRATED: 31 October

♦ ALSO KNOWN AS: Halloween or All Hallows' Eve

Our ancestors used to split the year into two parts—the lighter half (summer) and the darker half (winter). The word "Samhain" means summer's end and traditionally marked the end of the season of light and the beginning of the season of dark.

This was commonly considered the Celtic (and later—and still to this day—witches') new year, as our ancestors knew that all things begin from endings—so it was in the death of the harvest that a new one would form. They did not fear the dark and death, but instead saw this ending of summer as a new beginning. They understood that next year's good harvest started here, where the darkness allowed the earth to rest, regenerate, and prepare. They honored the year gone by and all it produced, and they gathered in the final resources that would last through winter. They also honored their ancestors, believing that the veils between worlds were thin, and those who had passed over could return to visit and impart wisdom.

Bonfires and lanterns were lit to lead spirits home, and places laid at the table for them during the feast. Because the veils were so thin, other spirits, faeries, and mischief-makers could also get through, so people wore costumes and masks to disguise and protect themselves, so that they would be mistaken for fellow spirits and therefore be left alone. The story goes that people would hide behind their disguises and play pranks on each other, blaming the spirits—a tradition that continues in our Halloween celebrations to this day, in the form of trick or treating.

Samhain became All Saints' Day and later Halloween, but many of the Samhain traditions lived on.

SPEND SAMHAIN WITH YOUR SOUL

Halfway between the autumn equinox and winter solstice, Samhain is the cross-quarter festival that celebrates the end of autumn and marks the first signs of winter. It is a turning point that takes us deeper into the inwardly-focused period of rest and stillness, honoring the death of the old and, with that, the promise of rebirth.

This is the time to look at what needs to be allowed to die away and end in your life—not necessarily for good, but in its current version—in order that something new can grow in its place.

As the day when the veils between the worlds are said to be at their thinnest, Samhain also helps us to move deeper into our intuition and the world of inner knowing—the things we can't logically understand but we just "know." It is a time to embrace the darkness, to explore and know ourselves and our inner mysteries and the power and potential that lie within us. We can also use the dark time of year to face fears, look at what we have been avoiding seeing, and embrace our shadows, so alchemizing them into magic.

SAMHAIN RITUALS

Set time aside in the days around Samhain to dedicate to these ritual practices and make the most of this seasonal transition.

Let parts of you die away to be reborn

Which parts of you are you finally ready to let go of? Maybe it's the people-pleaser in you, parts of your past, shame that keeps you small, fears that keep you stuck, heartbreak that keeps your heart closed, or self-doubts that limit you?

In their place, what do you want to nurture in yourself over winter, so that you can be reborn? Perhaps more self-worth and self-belief? A promise to show up or speak up more? Embracing and welcoming in more of your shadows and turning toward your fears? A connection to your intuition, or a belief in your magic?

Hold a mini ritual where you honor and say goodbye to the parts you are ready to let go of. Thank them for their lessons and for trying to protect you, but let them know you don't need them any more. Then welcome in your new parts and think of ways in which you can begin to embrace and nurture them over winter.

Honor your ancestors

Think of all those in your life who have gone before you and take time to honor and celebrate their lives and the ways they touched yours. This is also a powerful time to look at any repeating patterns of behavior in your family lineage or beliefs, and how you can be the one to end these and do things differently.

Honor the cycle of death and rebirth

Take some time here to honor not only loved ones who have died, but any other deaths that have happened in your life. Often, we don't give ourselves the opportunity to grieve the ending of things like relationships, jobs, friendships, dreams that we never followed, and directions we didn't go in. Mark any big turning points in your life, so that you can grieve them, take lessons from them, and then leave them in the past.

SAMHAIN JOURNAL PROMPTS

♦ What have you been avoiding seeing or admitting about your life?

♦ What parts of your life need to die away so that they can be reborn?

- What turning points have happened in your life that you need to honor, grieve, and learn from?

- Where are you hiding in the shadows and concealing parts of yourself?

- What is magical about you? What can you offer to the world that no one else can?

- How are you going to reclaim your magic, power, and worth?

Sacred Season Made Simple

Nature is inspiring you to surrender and retreat into your inner world.

Reflect on what you need to say goodbye to.

Use the alchemical, magical energies of Scorpio season to listen to your intuition and remember your magic and power.

Samhain will help you to honor the cycles of life, death and rebirth, and embrace the darkness.

A moment of reflection

What have you learned about this season, and how can you apply it to your own life? How are you being called to shed, release, and complete things in your life, so that they can be reborn? What can you do to turn your awareness inwards and explore your inner world?

Reflect on the last season; did you do what you committed to doing?

This season I commit to:

_____

_____

_____

_____

CHAPTER 14

End-of-autumn Season —the Sacred Season for Journeying Inwards

DATES: 22 November–20 December

WHEEL-OF-THE-YEAR CELEBRATION: none

ZODIAC SEASON: Sagittarius

MOONS THIS SEASON: Sagittarius new moon and Gemini full moon

REFLECT THIS SEASON ON: how you can take care of yourself while still enjoying all this season has to offer, exploring your inner world.

LOOK OUT IN NATURE FOR: starlings and robins; Nature in her still, quiet presence, as everything retreats into hibernation.

The end of autumn brings us Sagittarius season to help us transition seasons and venture into the unknown, as the darkness of winter takes hold. We are entering the deepest, darkest depths of the year, with frosty days and cold, dark nights.

All is barren and bare, and there is a stillness in the air, as all of Nature has retreated deep within into hibernation, stillness, and rest. And just as Nature hibernates so as to slow down and save energy to survive the winter, we are called to do the same.

Yet this is often the season when we do the exact opposite, filling our days and nights with events, parties, and shopping for the festive season. We try to come to life when the world around us retreats, and I honestly believe that's why so many people are left feeling frazzled, exhausted, and run down at this time of year. With all its twinkly lights, festivities, and a certain magic in the air, Christmas is a time to be embraced and enjoyed. But take inspiration from Nature, too, and balance out the busyness with conscious time alone—resting, going within, and just being—and you'll enjoy all that this season has to offer so much more.

A sacred pause

Take a sacred pause here in arguably one of the busiest times of year to notice where you are doing too much and giving too much to the outside world, leaving yourself and your inner world depleted. Use this time of slowing down to avoid burnout, making sure that you take care of your own needs, too.

Fill yourself up from the inside by making conscious time for stillness, silence, and listening to your inner world, and this will ensure that you have the energy to enjoy all that this season has to offer.

JOURNAL PROMPTS FOR THE SACRED PAUSE

♦ Are you doing and giving too much?

♦ How can you nurture your inner world more
  and take care of your own needs?

♦ How can you enjoy this season
  without burning out?

End-of-autumn Altar

Add earthy colors to your altar, such as brown or dark green; or the colors of the festive season, such as red, silver, and gold.

Gather twigs, dried leaves, and dried earth to remind yourself of this time of stillness, hibernation, and returning to the earth.

Place representations of what you are visualizing for yourself for the coming year ahead on your altar, and some festive cheer, as cues to make the most of this season, whatever that means for you. Add reminders of the importance of taking care of yourself at this time of year. This could be little Post-its prompting you to nurture yourself and to remember what this season is about, beyond the consumerism.

End-of-autumn Daily Rituals

Embrace these daily rituals to help you connect to the essence of this season and Nature's guidance.

DAILY CHECK-IN

Pause at the beginning of each day and check in with how you are feeling and what you need right now. You may also do this throughout the day, or whenever you catch yourself in a place of overwhelm. It will help you to stay connected to your inner world, in touch with what you need and to catch any burnout before it happens.

DO ONE ACT OF SELF-CARE A DAY

This may be a long bubble bath, an early night, time in the dark watching your Christmas tree lights twinkle, a movie with mince pies, or just knowing when to say no to invites. Do one thing daily, even if it's just for five minutes, to fill up your tank and ensure that you're keeping your inner world warm and nurtured.

JOURNEY INWARDS

Spend time journeying inwards, like Nature. Get to know yourself better through meditation, contemplation, or journaling. Get curious about your way of thinking, viewpoints, personal values, and identity. Study and explore your inner world this season and see what you discover.

Crystals for the End of Autumn

◆ HEMATITE This will help you to remain grounded and connected to yourself and your needs, and will keep you in the present, rather than getting lost in the busyness all around you.

◆ LAPIS LAZULI A seeker of truth, lapis will help you to explore your inner world and bring self-awareness, knowledge, and meaning into your life.

Affirmations for the End of Autumn

◆ "I know who I am."

◆ "I take care of myself and my needs."

◆ "I enjoy all that this season has to offer."

Ways to Work with Sagittarius Season

Moving you out of the shadows of Scorpio, Sagittarius will help you to expand your horizons and embrace both sides of this season. As a sign that continually seeks to find the meaning of life and increase understanding and consciousness, Sagittarius will encourage you to go within, like Nature, and explore your inner world and what makes you tick.

At the same time, Sagittarius brings an energy boost and a hit of inspiration, optimism, and positivity to get you through the end of the year. So use Sagittarius's adventurous spirit to seize the moment and explore all the joy that the season has to offer.

USE SAGITTARIUS SEASON TO...

♦ ...FIND YOUR PERSONAL FREEDOM. For some people, the thought of weeks of parties and celebrations lights them all the way up, while others are filled with dread. Sagittarius wants you to be in your full expression and feel free to be who you are. Embrace the JOMO (joy of missing out) and stay snuggled up indoors if that's more your vibe—and do it with pride. Be true to you and don't give in to pressure.

♦ ...PLAN AN ESCAPE. As the eternal wanderer, Sagittarius wants to feel free to adventure and explore. This may mean that you ditch the upcoming winter and head for sunnier climes; or just wrap up, get outside, and explore walks, parks, and Nature trails near you. Either way, make sure you take yourself on some kind of escape this season and you'll feel so much better for it.

♦ ...BEGIN TO ENVISION NEXT YEAR. Sagittarius season brings a sense of optimism and expansion, and a feeling that anything is possible, so use it to look toward what you want your future to hold. What have you learned about yourself and life this year and how do you want to use this wisdom to do things differently going forwards? Imagine you could have anything you wanted for yourself next year—what would that be? Start to envision all that the year ahead holds.

End-of-autumn Moons

The end-of-autumn season brings us the Sagittarius new moon and Gemini full moon.

THE SAGITTARIUS NEW MOON

The Sagittarius new moon will help you to see the light within the dark of this season, and to take what you've learned and turn it into a new vision and dream.

This is the last full lunar cycle of the year and gives you a real opportunity to review and reflect on the year gone by, what it has taught you and how you've grown. This is a season to get out of your comfort zone, believe in yourself, and go after your true north and what you want. This is a new moon for action—for acknowledging where you are and knowing where you want to be.

Mini new-moon ritual

Sagittarius prepares us for change, so use this new moon to get honest about the changes you'd like to make in your own life. Journal on whether what you thought you wanted at the start of the year is still what you want now. You are allowed to change your mind at any time, so use this moon to realize any changes that need to be made and embrace the freedom to be who you are and to do things differently next year.

THE GEMINI FULL MOON

All full moons bring a moment of completion and release, but this one does so in particular, as she's the final full moon before the winter solstice and turn of seasons.

The moon in Gemini takes us up into our heads and there can be a lot of confusion, questioning, anxiety, and heightened emotion. She will help you to seek a deeper meaning in your life and show you what is possible for you for the year ahead, and will bring the download of inspiration, insight, and ideas that you need to move forwards—but you need to be able to filter this out amid the noise.

It's important at this moon to slow down and take time to process all the information coming to you. To feel into what's true for you. One of the best ways to do this is to keep dropping out of your head and into the wisdom in your body—your intuitive wisdom.

Mini full-moon ritual

Meditate under this full moon to access your inner wisdom and guidance. Set a timer for ten to fifteen minutes, close your eyes, and place one hand on your belly and the other on your heart. Take long, slow, deep breaths all the way down into your belly. Feel everything around you slow down as you take your awareness deeper inwards with each breath. Now imagine that your body holds a profound wisdom. Listen to that. If your body could talk to you right now, what would it say? What insights and guidance does your body wisdom have to share with you?

How to Connect with Nature and Her Wisdom

Wrap up and get outside; walk in Nature and feel the stillness, the quiet, the deep levels of rest, and the healing power of slowing down. Listen to the crunch of Nature underfoot, take in your frost-covered surroundings, and see your breath on the air. Observe Nature in her raw, naked, beautiful state—a precious reminder, especially at this time of year, that we actually need so little.

Make time, though, to enjoy the other side of this year, too, perhaps choosing to gift time with loved ones instead of presents. Find little villages covered in twinkly lights, wander leisurely through Christmas markets, see huge trees covered in ornaments, recapture the essence of peace, love, and community that this time of year is truly about.

Watch for the spectacular sight of starling murmurations—a swooping mass of thousands of birds swirling together in the sky just before dusk. It's thought they do this for safety in numbers before descending to a communal roosting ground, where they

Sacred Season Made Simple

Nature is inspiring you to balance out busyness and doing with resting and being.

Reflect on where you're giving too much away to the outside world, leaving yourself and your inner world depleted.

Use the freedom-loving energies of Sagittarius to embrace this season, whatever that may mean for you.

share information about feeding areas and huddle together to keep warm. This beautiful display is a wonderful reminder of sharing and working together for common goals.

Look out for robins, too—a favorite animal associated with this time of year. With their bright red breasts, they are not only a sign of hope, new beginnings, and happiness but are said by some to be loved ones who have passed and are now coming to pay a visit. Say hello to any robins you meet and see if they have any messages for you.

A moment of reflection

What have you learned about this season, and how can you apply it to your own life? How are you being called to go inwards and take care of your inner world? What do you need to do to enjoy and make the most of this season, while also taking care of yourself?

Reflect on the last season; did you do what you committed to doing?

This season I commit to:

_____

_____

_____

_____

THE SACRED SEASON OF

Winter

START-OF-WINTER SEASON: 21 December–19 January—the sacred season for looking to the light (pp. 183–196)

MID-WINTER SEASON: 20 January–18 February—the sacred season for awakening (pp. 197–210)

END-OF-WINTER SEASON: 19 February–20 March—the sacred season for endings and beginnings (pp. 211–220)

CHAPTER 15

Start-of-winter Season —the Sacred Season for Looking to the Light

DATES: 21 December–19 January

WHEEL-OF-THE-YEAR CELEBRATION: winter solstice, approx. 21 December

ZODIAC SEASON: Capricorn

MOONS THIS SEASON: Capricorn new moon and Cancer full moon

REFLECT THIS SEASON ON: gathering your inner resources, taking rest, and beginning to welcome back the light.

LOOK OUT IN NATURE FOR: the stillness of everything in deep hibernation and the signs of eternal life in the evergreens.

The start of winter brings us the winter solstice, Capricorn season, and the season when Nature has withdrawn into deep, silent rest.

Winter has taken hold. The days are cold and short, the nights are dark and long, and Nature is well and truly tucked away in her inner world—sleeping, resting, recuperating, and conserving energy for the lighter days ahead.

Very little seems to be happening on the outside in Nature, but beneath the earth, vast systems of roots are gathering nutrients, so that there will be enough energy for growth in spring. And this is when we too should be preparing for the year ahead—not by forcing ourselves out into the world, but by gathering our inner resources and taking rest.

Many of us try to fight against Nature at this time of year; we are already exhausted after December festivities, yet we push ourselves out there into a cold, dark world, to hit the ground running—when it is likely still hard and frozen over. I think that's why many of us slip up in January or are at least exhausted by the time the year and Nature begin to truly come to life.

How much more in flow would we be if we granted ourselves the grace of pausing, retreating, and resting in January? If we turned our awareness to true self-care and laying the inner groundwork for the year ahead through self-reflection, self-awareness, and giving ourselves what we need to be able to grow into the best we can be.

Although we're in the deepest, darkest depths of winter, this season brings us the longest night and the shortest day, meaning that lighter days are coming. This is our reminder that the dark times do not last forever and the light is always there, waiting to break through again.

So enjoy these last few weeks of peaceful hibernation; go within and gather what you need, so that you are ready for the lighter days ahead.

A sacred pause

Take a sacred pause here to set the tone for the rest of the traditional year ahead. Do you want it to begin with restrictions, to-do lists, and a sense of overwhelm, so that you are constantly rushing and running on empty? Or do you want to enter the year feeling calm, at peace, and connected to yourself, committed to taking care of yourself and moving through the year with trust, ease, and flow?

Set resolutions for future you, if that feels right. Focus on laying the foundations for what you need to be doing to look after and take care of yourself, so that future you has the energy and resources needed to make these things happen in your life.

JOURNAL PROMPTS FOR THE SACRED PAUSE

♦ What do you want the theme to be for the year ahead?

♦ How can you take good care of yourself this January?

♦ Are you setting any resolutions for future you? What do you need to be doing now to make sure these can happen?

Start-of-winter Altar

Red, green, gold, and white are the colors of this season.

Make sure to add a candle to welcome back the light. Adorn your altar with evergreens, like holly, ivy, and mistletoe. Create your own yule log or even a wreath. Add symbols of the returning sun and things that represent what you want to bring into the year ahead.

Start-of-winter Daily Rituals

Embrace these daily rituals to help you connect to the essence of this season and Nature's guidance.

WELCOME BACK THE LIGHT

Light a candle each day to symbolically invite the light back into your life. Spend a few moments gazing into the flame, welcoming in love, laughter, joy, new beginnings, and anything else you wish to come into your life.

SPEND TIME IN SILENCE

Embrace the stillness of this season by spending time each day in silent reflection. Use this time to tune into and honor the stillness that winter brings and the slower, quieter energy.

Especially at this time of year, silence will help you to slow down, recharge your mind, and center yourself amid the festive rush. Spending time in silence is scientifically proven to reduce stress levels and blood pressure, boost your brain chemistry, regulate hormones, and, most importantly for this time of year, boost your immune system. You may even choose to honor the turning point of the year by spending the day of the winter solstice in contemplative silence.

EMBRACE ENCHANTMENT

Remember how you felt as a child at this time of year, when everything seemed magical, enchanting, and filled with wonder and delight? Adult life can sometimes leave us feeling a little jaded, especially with long to-do lists and a lot of pressure. So why not invite more enchantment into your daily life? Try to view this season with childlike wonder; take time to enjoy and appreciate festive celebrations and capture the spirit of love and magic.

Crystals for the Start of Winter

♦ SNOW QUARTZ This brings a childlike innocence that can allow you to see and appreciate the wonders of this time of year. It heightens your intuition, helping you to listen within and connect to your inner knowing.

♦ CITRINE This will help you to welcome back the light and move into the new year connected to your inner power, inner sunshine, and sense of self-worth.

Affirmations for the Start of Winter

♦ "I listen to my needs and take care of myself."

♦ "I am light."

♦ "I move into the year ahead with intention and purpose."

Ways to Work with Capricorn Season

Taking you from the exploration of Sagittarius season, Capricorn season comes to help you plan ahead for the coming year.

Even though we are still in the darkness of winter, Capricorn energy is long-term and future-focused, helping you look forwards.

This season will allow you to recognize what is stirring in your soul and what you are being pulled toward at the beginning of the traditional year, creating the theme of this next year for you.

As an earth sign, Capricorn doesn't want you to just dream and set intentions for the year ahead, but to be pragmatic. This sign will bring the discipline, resources, and practical steps needed to look to the future and take inspired action toward your goals.

USE CAPRICORN SEASON TO...

♦ ...EXPAND YOUR HORIZONS. With the colder, darker nights, winter is a wonderful time to take your focus inwards and study not only yourself, but also something new, which will inspire the year ahead for you. Take the opportunity to get a qualification, take a course, learn a new skill, reignite your passion for a certain hobby, read books on topics that interest you and expand your mind.

♦ ...LIVE ON PURPOSE. Capricorn is the sign associated with purpose, so use this season to invite more of that into your daily life. Drink your morning coffee with purpose, find purpose in the work you are doing, make decisions on purpose, trust that every challenge that comes along has a purpose. Begin to live as though your every thought, word, and action is on purpose, and watch your life take on more meaning.

♦ ...PLAN YOUR YEAR AHEAD. Get a wall planner or a year planner and look ahead to what you want to do, create, and make happen this year. What do you need to be doing and putting in place now to make sure that these things can be realized in your future? Make lists, formulate a plan, and get organized.

Start-of-winter Moons

The start-of-winter season brings us the Capricorn new moon and Cancer full moon.

THE CAPRICORN NEW MOON

With the moon in Capricorn, it's time to get clear on where you are going this year, and how you are going to get there. This moon is about creating lasting change through consistency, commitment, and planning for the traditional year ahead. She helps you to lay the foundations for the year, so that you may envision and commit to what you want, and brings the practical means for you to get it.

Mini new-moon ritual

Look ahead. Where do you want to be in a year's time?

Get a clear idea of what you would like the next year to bring you, what you want to achieve and any simple changes you can begin to make now to realize your dreams. Break your dreams up into clear, manageable steps that you can take every day, week, and month to move you forwards toward what you want.

THE CANCER FULL MOON

All full moons are a time of closure and completion, but this watery full moon comes along to help you process the year gone by, realize the lessons, and leave behind anything that you don't want to carry into the new year with you.

You may feel a lot of emotion around this full moon, but she will cleanse and release, washing away the year, and there will be insights and power that come from diving into your emotional depths. Because it's only by allowing yourself to really feel into and process the year that you will be able to release it and make room for what's next. Your way forward will be lit up by the heartfelt guidance of this nurturing, intuitive, loyal, and supportive full moon.

Mini full-moon ritual

Use this moon to process, learn from, heal, and release the year gone by. Reflect on each month of the last year, one at a time, taking note of anything left unfinished or unhealed, what you learned and achieved, as well as what the year as a whole offered you. See the blessings and the lessons, then close off the year and turn from the past to the future.

How to Connect with Nature and Her Wisdom

One of my favorite ways to welcome the light back in at this time of year is to get outside and greet the sunrise. The light is spectacular and you get to witness Nature easing herself out of slumber a little more each day, inspiring you to do the same.

Wrap up, get outside, and walk in silence as often as you can. Allow Nature to inspire you with her stillness. Open all your senses and really immerse yourself in her. See how she has shed everything, let go, laid herself bare, and gone fully within. Nature has no fear of missing out or need for constant outside stimulation. Feel the power that she radiates from her withdrawal and stillness.

Look out for mistletoe, holly, and ivy—three evergreen plants with long associations with winter and, very often, the only green signs of life and survival in Nature over the dark winter months.

Mistletoe can usually be found growing in the branches of host trees. It has long associations with the winter solstice, having been a favorite of the druids; legend has it that on the sixth night after the new moon following the winter solstice, they would cut it from the oak with a golden sickle, catch it with a white cloak, then give it to villagers for protection, and use in fertility rituals. Ivy is often found wrapped around trees and just about anything it can climb, tolerating tough conditions, and showing us how to keep going, even when things feel impossible. As it grows back after being cut, it is a symbol of rebirth, everlasting life, and fertility. The druids considered ivy the feminine, whereas holly was the masculine. You'll find holly in hedgerows and oak and beech woodland. Holly was again used for protection and fertility, symbolizing eternal life.

The Winter Solstice

- ◆ DATE CELEBRATED: approximately 21 December

- ◆ ALSO KNOWN AS: Yule

The return of the sun and warmer, lighter days would have been a significant moment for many ancient cultures, as they rejoiced at having survived the winter. This was the merry season, when everyone feasted, danced, and drank in celebration.

Traditionally, Yule was said to have been marked for twelve days, possibly as our ancestors believed that the sun stood still for twelve days in the middle of the winter. A Yule log (in England, this would likely have been oak or ash) was lit to banish the darkness and celebrate the return of the sun and light. Then the ashes were said to be planted in the soil for good luck and used for fertility rituals. Houses were adorned with evergreens to encourage the return of summer and the sun; and outdoors, trees were decorated with ornaments, gifts, and candles to urge them to return in the spring. Wreaths were made and hung on doors to symbolize the completion of another cycle, and holly and mistletoe were hung for protection and to represent hope and fertility.

Wassailing was a Twelfth-Night tradition where people would visit orchards and sing to the trees to ask for a good harvest the following year.

Here the Holly King reigns and is at his full power (see p. 112) before surrendering to the Oak King at the Spring Equinox, when the light and sun truly begin to return.

Yule later became Christmas, but as you can see, many of the ancient traditions remained.

SPEND THE WINTER SOLSTICE WITH YOUR SOUL

The winter solstice is the shortest day and longest night of the year, when we have reached the depths of the darkness, after which the days begin to lengthen and we welcome back the light of the sun.

The winter solstice has long been a significant time of reflection and ritual. It's a time to look back over what the depths of winter taught you and begin to emerge from the darkness, looking forwards to the sun's returning power, and using its light to consciously manifest what you want to create.

It is the perfect time to pause and reflect upon the past year and what it brought you; a natural time to say goodbye to the old before welcoming in the new; an ending to create a new beginning.

As the sun begins to return, it's also a beautiful time to reflect on the light that fills your life and how you're being called to shine your light more as you begin a new cycle and year ahead.

WINTER-SOLSTICE RITUALS

Set time aside in the days around the winter solstice to dedicate to these ritual practices and make the most of this seasonal transition.

Reflect on the year gone by

Take an honest assessment of the past year and how far you have come. Take note of what worked and what didn't, whether you did all the things you set out to achieve at the start of the year, and what the year brought for you in general.

If you feel that you are holding on to any resentments, hurts, and regrets from the past year, write them down on pieces of paper, then burn them. As you do so, affirm that you are willing to let go and symbolically feel the cleansing effect of the fire, releasing all these things from your life.

Take a mini hibernation retreat

Just as Nature hibernates over winter, this is the ideal time for you to do the same. Set aside an entire day (or as much time as you can) when you will be undisturbed and, ideally, alone—a time when you have no commitments, nowhere to go, and nothing else you need to be doing—and use this time to hibernate.

Draw your energy inwards, take care of, and nourish yourself and leave the outside world behind for just a day, so you can re-energize and recharge. This is especially important at this time of year with all the demands of the festive season, which can often leave us feeling stressed and drained. Taking this small amount of time out for yourself will help you to re-emerge as a brand-new you, able to shine your light, and offer so much more to all those around you.

Learn from the darkness to shine your light

We all have periods of darkness in our lives, but these can be the times we really learn from. Reflect on your most painful experiences and what they have taught you. Often, they bring you the most insight, awareness, lessons, and growth. Can you see the purpose in your pain and use it to emerge from the darkness, like Nature, stronger, more resilient, and powerful?

Then write down what you have to offer the world: all the ways in which you shine and light up the lives of those around you, and how you can allow yourself to shine more and share more of your unique light out into the world.

WINTER-SOLSTICE JOURNAL PROMPTS

- ♦ What have you learned from the darkness of winter, and the darker times in your life?

- ◆ What has been your biggest challenge this year? How did you overcome it and/or what did it teach you?

- ◆ What has been your greatest achievement this year and/or what are you most proud of yourself for?

- ◆ What brings the most light to your life?

- ◆ How can you allow yourself to shine more? How are you being called to shine your unique beautiful light out into the world?

- ◆ What do you want to consciously create in your life for the next cycle and into the next year?

Sacred Season Made Simple

Nature is inspiring you to go inwards into deep, silent rest and hibernation.

Reflect the on tone you want to set and how you want to move into the coming year.

Use the long-term future-focused energies of Capricorn season to expand your horizons and plan the year ahead.

The winter solstice will help you to learn from the depths of winter and look toward the return of the light.

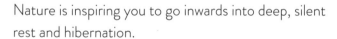

A moment of reflection

What have you learned about this season, and how can you apply it to your own life? How are you being called to balance out this busy time of year with more inner stillness, silence, and reflection? How can you take your lessons from the winter and begin to welcome back the light in your own life?

Reflect on the last season; did you do what you committed to doing?

This season I commit to:

_____

_____

_____

_____

CHAPTER 16

Mid-winter Season —the Sacred Season for Envisioning and Emerging

DATES: 20 January–18 February

WHEEL-OF-THE-YEAR CELEBRATION: Imbolc, 1/2 February

ZODIAC SEASON: Aquarius

MOONS THIS SEASON: Aquarius new moon and Leo full moon

REFLECT THIS SEASON ON: what is stirring within you wanting to awaken, the wisdom you gained over winter, and what seeds you want to plant for spring.

LOOK OUT IN NATURE FOR: snowdrops beginning to push through the earth, primroses appearing, and the song thrush starting to sing.

This can often seem to be the hardest part of what feels like an eternal winter; it's generally the coldest, the iciest, and the season we most likely get snow, and we're all a bit winter-weary by now.

Then, all of a sudden, we see the first signs of life pushing through the earth, reminding us that nothing lasts forever—not even winter.

Nature gives us hope of all that is yet to come. This is the season when she rouses very gently beneath the surface, as though taking a little stretch and starting to tentatively think about coming out of hibernation. And just as the seeds that have been buried deep within the soil over winter begin to stir, you will feel things gently stirring within you, too.

This is a seemingly conflicting time of creation and one of patience, which is something Nature can teach us all about: winter isn't over, yet we are seeing the first signs of spring, and it can be tempting now to want to rush winter away and skip to the good part. But while there is the promise of spring, the seeds aren't quite ready to break the surface yet, and both we and Nature must use this time of germination to give our seeds the best chance of coming into full growth when the time is right.

So for now, it's time to gently stretch alongside Nature and, taking what we've learned in hibernation, start to envision what the future holds and what we want to awaken in ourselves and our lives as spring comes along.

A sacred pause

As the first signs of life begin to emerge in Nature, take a sacred pause to look at what you have learned through the depths of winter and hibernation, and who you want to emerge as come spring.

In this liminal time between seasons, you, Nature, and the sun are experiencing a rebirth. This is a beautiful opportunity to get to know who you want to be and reintroduce yourself to the outside world, before it gets busy and takes over, telling you who you need to be.

It is a time to see how you've changed and grown, and what you no longer want to do, be or accept in your life as you emerge into spring.

JOURNAL PROMPTS FOR THE SACRED PAUSE

♦ How have you changed and grown over winter?

♦ What have been your biggest lessons over the last few months?

♦ Reintroduce yourself: who are you emerging as?

Mid-winter Altar

White, green, and pink are the colors associated with Imbolc and the middle of winter, so adorn your altar with them.

Add images or symbols of who you are emerging out of winter as, who you are growing into, and what you want to grow in your life in spring.

Gather early spring flowers like snowdrops or plant some seeds in a pot and keep this on your altar to remind you of the importance of tending to them while they are beneath the earth.

Mid-winter Daily Rituals

Embrace these daily rituals to help you connect to the essence of this season and Nature's guidance.

STRETCH YOUR WAY INTO EACH DAY

Every morning, even if only for five minutes, do a simple stretch (you could even do it while you're still in bed). Tune into where in your body still feels sleepy, stuck, or restricted and gently stretch and move it awake. Trust your intuition and your body, which will help you to stay more inwardly connected as the world around you begins to wake up. Visualize coming out of your hibernation more and more each day, preparing body, mind, and heart for moving into spring.

MAKE SPACE

Allow space for what wants to come to life within you to make itself known to you. This may be following your stretching (above) with five minutes' meditation, or just sitting quietly and breathing;

or you may choose to dance or draw or lose yourself in painting or singing. Make space for new beginnings, too. Create as much space as you can in yourself and your life.

TURN INWARDS

Although the world is beginning to awaken, our attention is still inwardly focused, so as to manifest our desires within us.

Anything you want to see on the outside has to first come to life within you—just as a seed comes to life first beneath the earth. Go inwards daily, connect to your desires, and feel them alive inside you. If you want more love in your life, feel the love within you first; if you want more happiness, find happiness within you; if you want freedom, feel free. Whatever you want to create and grow in your outer world, first go inwards to find it there.

Crystals for Mid-winter

♦ SELENITE Selenite will help you to cleanse your body, mind, heart, and soul, and to listen to and trust the intuitive feelings of what wants to awaken within you and come to life in the year ahead.

♦ RUTILATED QUARTZ A crystal of soul growth, rutilated quartz will help you to go on a journey of self-discovery and self-awareness to know yourself and what you want, need, and desire.

Affirmations for Mid-winter

- ◆ "I create more space in my life."

- ◆ "I know who I am."

- ◆ "I trust what wants to awaken within me."

Ways to Work with Aquarius Season

With Capricorn having helped you to put plans in place for the year, Aquarius now comes to show you a future beyond winter and gives you a little glimmer of hope for all that is possible for you in the coming spring.

Aquarius brings with it a freedom-seeking quality, along with sparks of inspiration and clarity, new ideas, visions, and ways of looking at things. Use this season to discover and get to know more of yourself—more of what makes you you.

Aquarius energy teaches us that true freedom and liberation begin with us. As we give ourselves the freedom to be ourselves, live our truth, and follow our hearts, we give everyone around us permission and motivation to do the same.

This is a season to be you, to find a trust in yourself and the flow of life, to realign with your purpose, and create positive change to follow the direction of your dreams.

USE AQUARIUS SEASON TO...

- ◆ ...BREAK FREE FROM LIMITATIONS. The thing Aquarius loves most is freedom, so this is the season to look at where in your life you feel stuck, held down, and held back—bound not just by external factors but also by yourself.

♦ ...LOOK TOWARD THE FUTURE. Aquarius season gives you the opportunity to envision the bigger picture of your life, so use your imagination to visualize what you want from it—the kind of world that you want to live in and how you can make that happen.

♦ ...BE MORE YOU. No more pretending to be someone or something you're not and doing and saying the things expected of you. It's time to find the freedom to be authentically you—to love, accept, and embrace who you are and bring the fullest expression of yourself to the world.

Mid-winter Moons

The mid-winter season brings us the Aquarius new moon and Leo full moon.

THE AQUARIUS NEW MOON

Under this new moon, it's time to find the freedom to be yourself, and to step out into the world as you; to show yourself; and to contribute in the way that only you can. You are the main gift you have to offer the world; the reason you are here on earth—to be you. But you can only do this if you know who you are. So under this new moon, dig deep, get clear on who you are, and know your value and worth in the world. And if you are unclear, be authentic and passionate, and allow this moon to show you the rest.

Mini new-moon ritual

Spend time under this moon journaling on how you're being called to come out of your hibernation comfort zone and take risks into the unknown. Imagine that you fully believed that just like everything in Nature has a purpose, you do, too—what would your purpose be? Who are you here to be and what are you here to do?

THE LEO FULL MOON

The Leo full moon brings the fire—to move things along, to burn through all that's standing in the way, and to reignite your passions and desires.

This full moon brings a lot of energy, a lot of shifts, and a lot of heart. It may be an emotional ride, but if you can remain in your heart, trust the bigger picture and hold true to yourself, this moon will shine a light on a way forward through the year ahead.

This is a moon that wants you to be seen, acknowledged, and, most of all, fully accepted in your truest authenticity. No moon wants you to shine all of yourself more brightly and boldly into the world than a Leo moon.

Leo rules the heart, so listen to all that is in yours and all that prevents you from fully fulfilling your purpose and dreams.

Mini full-moon ritual

Hold a releasing ritual to help you let go of anything that stands in the way of making your Imbolc/spring wishes come true, ensuring that you are ready to move forwards.

Write down everything that's preventing you from fully opening your heart, following your wishes and dreams, and living up to your full potential. Write down all the doubts, fears, and stories that stand in your way, and ask the power of the Leo full moon to help you to release it all. When you are ready to let it go, burn the paper (safely) and visualize all these doubts and fears going up in flames and being carried away, leaving you ready to move forwards into new spring beginnings.

How to Connect with Nature and Her Wisdom

Spend time with the snowdrops—the ultimate sign of hope and the promise of good things to come. Think about what they have gone through to grow, pushing through the frozen, snow-covered ground. Growth is sometimes uncomfortable; it drives us to our edges, and it can be easy to give up. If you are currently facing challenges or anything that feels uncomfortable, let the snowdrops remind you of what is waiting on the other side.

This is the month when we will most likely experience snow, which, although sometimes inconvenient, brings us one of the most beautiful life lessons. Because every snowflake that falls is unique, no matter how many billions of them fall from the sky, no two will be the same. Watch the snow fall and realize the beauty of embracing your uniqueness, and how you, just like each and every snowflake, are perfect just the way you are.

Imbolc

♦ DATE CELEBRATED: 1/2 February

♦ ALSO KNOWN AS: Imbolg

The word Imbolc means "in the navel," which referred to the first signs of life emerging from the womb of Mother Earth and the fact that lactating animals began to give birth.

Over long, hard, bitter winters, many people simply didn't have enough to survive, so the first signs of spring beginning to appear through the frozen earth told them that they had almost made it through and must have been quite the cause for celebration.

As the sun's light began to increase, this was a festival of purification and cleansing, when people would wash away the dark of winter in preparation for welcoming the light.

Imbolc is a fire festival that was associated with Brigid, goddess of the sacred fire who brings fertility, wisdom, and healing, and teaches how to nurture the land. Thanks, and prayers were offered to her to bless the household and home, and bring abundance and fertility for the coming year. Lamps were lit and bonfires set alight to honor Brigid and welcome the returning sun. Small dolls were made of straw and taken from house to house to bless and protect people's homes.

Water was also associated with Brigid, for its cleansing properties, and it was traditional to visit sacred wells at Imbolc to leave an offering and say a prayer to the goddess.

Brigid later became St. Brigid and Imbolc became Candlemas.

SPEND IMBOLC WITH YOUR SOUL

Imbolc is the cross-quarter festival that celebrates the first emergence out of winter toward spring. It begins at sunset on 1 February and continues through to sunset on 2 February. It is the halfway point between the winter solstice and spring equinox, and is a time for listening to the inner wisdom you gained over your winter hibernation and tuning into the manifestation potential of spring.

Imbolc stirs all the seeds of life that have been buried deep within the soil—and within you—over winter, asking you to begin to inwardly prepare for the shift in season and a re-emergence out into the world in spring.

You are not yet out of hibernation, but you're no longer still sleeping. You're in that dreamlike state between the two, when you are most in tune with your dreams and can access your inner world.

Search within for the wisdom you need to find your way forward, as you begin to gently shake off winter and look toward the faint glimmer of spring. Look at how you've changed and what you learned over winter, what you want to bring out of hibernation with you, and what you want to put into action over spring.

IMBOLC RITUALS

Set time aside in the days around Imbolc to dedicate to these ritual practices and make the most of this seasonal transition.

Gather your winter wisdom

On the evening of Imbolc, take some time to write down all that you have learned over winter, all the lessons and learnings and wisdom you have gained.

Take note of what you want to leave behind as you emerge from hibernation, and what new insights and wisdom you want to take forwards into the coming year.

Honor all that you have learned over winter and the wisdom you have gained, so that you can use it to move out of winter and into spring.

Look toward the season ahead

Now take what you learned through your winter hibernation and use it to decide what you want to grow in the year ahead. Knowing what you now know, how do you want to do things differently this year?

Write down everything that is stirring within you—all the dreams, ideas, and what you would like to make happen in your life and see grow over spring and summer. Feel these seeds alive within you and remember that now is not yet the time for action, but simply a time to allow your seeds to germinate within you and take root. Think about what you can be doing now to nourish them, so that they are ready to grow when the time comes.

Emerge out of winter

It was traditional at Imbolc to light every lamp in the house at sunset to welcome Brigid's energy. You can follow this ancient practice by mindfully lighting all the lamps in your home at sunset, or simply lighting a candle to welcome back the light. Symbolically feel yourself moving out of hibernation and taking that first step forwards toward the light and spring.

This was also a time for visiting holy wells or springs to purify and cleanse away the old to welcome in the new. If there is a fresh stream near you (or if you can face the sea at this time of year), go and get your hands and feet in the water and splash it over you, asking the water to cleanse and purify you. Or, if that's too much, take a ritual bath or shower and feel the water washing away the remnants of winter, leaving you ready to emerge into spring.

IMBOLC JOURNAL PROMPTS

- ◆ What has been your greatest lesson from the winter season?

- ◆ What has been your biggest challenge over the winter season?

- ◆ What did you learn about yourself over winter?

♦ What have you been holding on to over winter that you are ready to shake off and let go of?

♦ What have you been hiding from over winter that you are ready to face?

♦ What is stirring within you, wanting your attention?

Sacred Season Made Simple

Nature is inspiring you to gently stretch and stir back to life.

Reflect on what you learned through winter and who you want to emerge as in spring.

Use the liberating Aquarius energies to find the freedom to be you.

Imbolc will help you to listen to your inner wisdom and plant seeds for spring.

A moment of reflection

What have you learned about this season, and how can you apply it to your own life? How are you being called to take what you have learned over winter and use it to move forwards toward spring? What can you do to tend to your inner seeds and give everything that you want the best chance to grow?

Reflect on the last season; did you do what you committed to doing?

This season I commit to:

_____

_____

_____

_____

End-of-winter Season —the Sacred Season for Endings and Beginnings

✳

DATES: 19 February–20 March

WHEEL-OF-THE-YEAR CELEBRATION: none

ZODIAC SEASON: Pisces

MOONS THIS SEASON: Pisces new moon and Virgo full moon

REFLECT THIS SEASON ON: forging a connection to your inner world, slowly shaking off winter and looking forwards, to what you want.

LOOK OUT IN NATURE FOR: the first signs of life beginning to stir, daffodils dancing, trees beginning to bud, and catkins hanging from the trees.

The end of winter brings us Pisces season, the final sign of the zodiac to help us to end winter.

The world around us is showing clear signs of coming back to life and giving us a glimpse of all that's to come as sap begins to rise, leaves appear on the trees, and daffodils dance on the breeze, all heralding the promise of spring and new beginnings.

After a deep, long rest, Nature is now finally shaking off and ending winter, but still, she doesn't rush. You don't see her go from barren to full bloom in a day; and likewise, we should take our time and move slowly into the season ahead.

Use this time to remain connected to your inner world and the stillness, silence, and peace you found within over winter, so that as the year begins to speed up again, you are in touch with yourself and what keeps you nourished from the inside. The seeds beneath the surface in Nature (and within you) hold the energy of a flower (and a dream) and will soon come to life. So there's no need to doubt or rush the process.

Like Nature, trust that the seeds stirring within you are going to come to life in perfect time. Don't rush them before they are ready; don't worry that it won't happen. Instead, hold the vision of what you want to create and dream it back to life.

Very soon, the world around you will speed up again—so before it bursts back to life, simply enjoy these last few dreamy weeks of quiet immersion and dreaming of what you want.

A sacred pause

As the season prepares to turn, take a sacred pause to check in with whether you are ready for what you want to grow in you and your life come spring.

Just as Nature can't grow anything in hard, old ground that hasn't been nurtured, neither can you. It's time now to prepare the inner soil of your heart and mind, so that you are ready for all that wants to grow and expand within you.

Look at where you are stuck in the past, or allowing limiting beliefs, doubts, and fears of what you are capable of to creep in. Use these last few weeks to loosen up your inner soil, dig out any old weeds, and fertilize your inner ground by trusting and believing in yourself and what you can achieve.

JOURNAL PROMPTS FOR THE SACRED PAUSE

- Where are you holding on to old resentments or the past?

- Are you ready for what you say you want? Is there space for it in your life?

- How can you prepare your inner world for what you want to grow?

End-of-winter Altar

Use light greens, yellow, and sky blue in your altar. Add daffodils, blackthorn, and early spring flowers as proof that Nature is coming back to life and inspiring you to do the same.

Add images, symbols, or representations of what is stirring within you, wanting to be brought to life, and what you want to create for yourself in the year ahead.

End-of-winter Daily Rituals

Embrace these daily rituals to help you connect to the essence of this season and Nature's guidance.

MOVE SLOWLY

Notice if you're already feeling a need to rush, and slow down instead. Don't let these first signs of spring fool you—you still have the whole year ahead of you. Be mindful, be intentional, and put practices in place now that will serve you through the rest of the year ahead; maybe a short pause or meditation in the morning before moving into your day, a breathing practice when you feel overwhelmed or just noticing when you get ten steps ahead of yourself and calling yourself back to the present.

FORGIVE DAILY

A forgiveness practice will help you to let go of the past and any resentments, and move forwards into a happier future. Remember that you forgive for yourself, not others—it is not about saying that what happened was right or ok, but that you no longer want to carry it with you. At the end of each day, scan it and forgive yourself and others for any wrongdoings—let them go with love.

LISTEN TO YOUR INTUITION

The first key to following your intuition is to listen, so make inner listening a daily habit. Any time you notice yourself trying to think your way to a solution or decision, try instead to get quiet and still, and listen to the wisdom in your body instead. Begin to feel more and think less. For example, cultivate an awareness of how decisions feel in your body, then commit to following through with what you are feeling.

Crystals for the End of Winter

◆ ROSE QUARTZ As one of the most healing crystals, rose quartz will help you to let go with love and forgiveness, and move on. It will also help you to love, accept, trust, and believe in yourself.

◆ MOONSTONE The crystal of new beginnings, moonstone reminds us of life's ever-changing rhythms and that all endings create new beginnings. Moonstone will help you to trust and connect to your intuition.

Affirmations for the End of Winter

◆ "I welcome endings to create new beginnings."

◆ "I trust my intuition and inner knowing."

◆ "I forgive and move on."

Ways to Work with Pisces Season

Aquarius season came to show you who you are, bringing the freedom to be you. Now Pisces season takes you into your inner world of intuition, feelings, hopes, and dreams, and what truly makes you happy.

You're still in hibernation, but Pisces season will help you to dream and envision what life looks like on the other side. Set time aside to daydream and let your imagination run free, and feel into all that's possible for you when spring arrives.

This is the season for trusting in something bigger, something greater, and that you are always being supported and guided in life.

Pisces season teaches you how to go with your own flow and to trust in you, in life, your emotions, your dreams, the call of your heart and soul, and the inner nudges of your intuition. And as the final sign of the zodiac, Pisces season comes to help you to find closure and completion, creating space for spring new beginnings.

USE PISCES SEASON TO...

♦ ...CREATE ENDINGS FOR NEW BEGINNINGS. Shed the old, release what doesn't serve you, tie up loose ends, and stop clinging on to and trying to control things that aren't working.

♦ ...FIND MORE TRUST. Trust in your intuition, the mystical and the magical. Try to listen more to the little inner voices within you and what they are trying to tell you, look out for signs guiding you, and live each day as though you are being supported by something greater. This will help you to develop more trust, not only in life, but also in yourself.

♦ ...PAY ATTENTION TO YOUR DREAMS. Pisces is the sign associated with dreams, making this the perfect time to start a dream journal. As soon as you wake up, write down as much as you remember from your dreams and how they made you feel; notice any themes, patterns, or signs, and what your subconscious may be trying to tell you.

End-of-winter Moons

The end-of-winter season brings us the Pisces new moon and Virgo full moon.

THE PISCES NEW MOON

As the new moon lands in the last sign of the zodiac, she completes the unraveling process of letting go of what is done and clearing space to allow in the new.

This dreamy new moon will give you the ability to envision and dream the future that you want for yourself. She's going to connect you to your highest wisdom and guidance, and show you the bigger picture of your life from your soul's perspective.

This moon wants you to create space for all the new beginnings that are coming, showing you a new part of you and a new stage of your life journey, both of which are ready to emerge.

Mini new-moon ritual

Take some time to dream. If you could have your dream life right now, what would that look like? Write down where you'd be, what you'd be doing, and who you'd be with. Go into as much detail as you can. Remember that you are never given a dream without also being given the means to achieve it. Under this moon it's time to find the dream.

THE VIRGO FULL MOON

The final one before the spring equinox, this full moon is a powerful portal for releasing and moving forwards.

As the healer of the zodiac, Virgo helps you to cleanse mentally, emotionally, and physically, so that you can move into spring and the start of the astrological year and truly start anew.

All full moons bring a heightened energy and emotion, but the lead-up to this one could be bumpy, as she shows you where you have held back from making change and avoided letting go of the comfortable, familiar, and what no longer serves you.

Mini full-moon ritual

Take a healing, cleansing ritual under this moon to release, clear, and let go.

Connect to the energies of this full moon bright in the sky above you. Visualize drawing moonlight down, in through the crown of your head and through your body. Ask this full moon to help cleanse you of anything that holds you back and sabotages you. Feel this moonlight move through your body, clearing everything away.

How to Connect with Nature and Her Wisdom

Spend time in Nature, watching her slowly begin to ease back to life, gradually emerging in preparation for the season ahead. There is no urgency; Nature doesn't push, rush, or force anything to be ready. Yet day by day, there will be a little more growth, as everything appears in its perfect time and in its perfect way. Let this inspire you to trust in the perfect unfolding of life.

The sight of daffodils is a reminder that the light is just around the corner now. These sunny flowers teach us one of the most beautiful lessons in this last season before spring: that part of us must be released and die for a new version of us to be born. Daffodils have a tough green skin around their blossoms to help them push through the cold, hard earth. As it gets warmer, the daffodil doesn't need this any more, so it shrivels and dies. Think about the protective layers you keep around yourself and whether it's time to let these fall away, too.

Sacred Season Made Simple

Nature is inspiring you to begin to slowly shake off winter and look at what you want to bring to life in the season ahead.

Reflect on whether you are ready and prepared for what you want to grow in your life.

Use the dreamy energy of Pisces to listen to your inner world and intuition, and create endings for new beginnings.

A moment of reflection

What have you learned about this season, and how can you apply it to your own life? How are you being called to prepare for what you want to bring to life over spring and summer? How can you cleanse and make way for the new?

Reflect on the last season; did you do what you committed to doing?

This season I commit to:

_____

_____

_____

_____

CONCLUSION

Thank you so much for taking this journey through the Sacred Seasons and the Wheel of the Year with me.

I hope that you have made self-discoveries and got to know yourself in a much deeper way.

Living in alignment with Nature and honoring not only her seasons and cycles, but also the seasons and cycles of my own life, has changed my life in immeasurable ways, and my wish is that it will be the same for you too.

I believe that we can find our true nature through Nature and be reminded of who we truly are, why we are here, and what life is all about.

Let this be a journey. Connect with Nature and let her show you the way.

I can't wait to see where this takes you...

I always love to hear from you, so please share your Nature wisdom and stories, tagging me on Instagram: @kirsty_gallagher_

ACKNOWLEDGMENTS

To my wonderful family: Sandra, Kylie, Kerry, Liam, Stephanie, Soraya, Jake, Chloe, Edward, Isaac, and my late Grandpa Donald. I love you all and thank you for always loving and supporting me.

To Sam for being the best friend a girl could ever ask for, and to my godson, Harley, and my Welsh family—thank you.

Thank you to Holly Whitaker and Liz Gough for your support and encouragement, and to all the wonderful people at Yellow Kite who have supported me on this journey. I am so grateful to Rebecca Mundy and Laura Bartholomew for your PR and marketing skills, Anne Newman for your editing magic and Jo Myler for creating yet another book cover of dreams.

If you are holding this book in your hands, thank you for allowing me to share Nature's wisdom with you. Nature has always been one of my greatest teachers and I hope that learning to live by her seasons transforms your life as much as it has mine. I always love to hear from you, so please do share your Nature magic by tagging me on Instagram @kirsty_gallagher_

Eternal gratitude to you if you bought my book *Lunar Living*, as you helped it become a *Sunday Times* bestseller—not just once, but three times! Thank you for all your support; you are the best community ever, and I appreciate you more than you know.

My Lunar Living online sisterhood: thank you for all your support, lunar love, and for being the best sisterhood there is. My never-ending gratitude goes to my right-hand woman, Helen Elias—nothing I do would be what it is without you.

To all of you who have attended my "Soul Space" online lunar yoga and meditation workshops, "Sacred Space" Wheel-of-the-Year workshops, and "Still Space" meditations, and to all my IG followers: thank you for being part of this magical community and continuing to show up for yourselves and each other. Remember, you are never alone; you've got this, I've got you, we've got each other.

Thank you to everyone at the *Chris Evans Breakfast Show* for all your support and allowing me to share the moon magic with the nation and at Car Fest. Thanks, too, to Fearne Cotton and *Happy Place*, Russell Brand, *You* magazine, *Red* magazine, *Stylist*, *Happiful* magazine, and everyone who has invited me on their podcasts to share my work.

If I have not named you, it's not because you have been forgotten or that I am not grateful. It's simply that I have been blessed to have so many wonderful people touch my life and not enough pages left to mention you all. It would be another book in itself! If you have ever been a part of my life in any way, thank you.

ABOUT THE AUTHOR

Kirsty Gallagher is a moon mentor, soul-alignment and spiritual coach, yoga teacher, meditation teacher, and *Sunday Times* best-selling author with an infectious passion for life.

She has been sharing the life-changing benefits of yoga and the moon for over 13 years through classes, workshops, and private and corporate sessions, and has taught over 80 worldwide retreats.

She is the author of the *Sunday Times* bestselling book *Lunar Living* and founder of the online sisterhood Lunar Living, which teaches how to weave the secret and ancient wisdom of the moon into modern, everyday life.

Kirsty has created a worldwide community through her Soul Space lunar yoga and meditation classes, and her Sacred Space seasonal yoga, meditation, and ritual classes. One of her greatest passions in life is bringing people together, showing us that we are never alone.

Kirsty works alongside women, teaching them to live back in alignment with an ancient cycle, a natural rhythm and flow, so helping them to connect back into their inner wisdom, power, authenticity, and purpose. Weaving lunar, Nature and divine feminine wisdom with spiritual teachings, astrology, and cutting-edge transformational coaching techniques, Kirsty helps women to overcome doubts, fears, and self-sabotage to know and trust in themselves like never before and find greater meaning and purpose in life.

Kirsty is a sought-after leading voice in lunar wisdom and has shared moon magic on *The Chris Evans Breakfast Show* and *This Morning*, is a contributor on Fearne Cotton's "Happy Place" app and festivals, and has been featured in *YOU*, *Stylist*, *Red*, *Women's Health*, *Soul & Spirit*, and *Natural Health* magazines.

Described as down to earth, warm-hearted, compassionate, and inspiring, Kirsty is known for bringing ancient mystical practices and wisdom to modern-day life in a relatable way that anyone and everyone can take something from.

Find out more at **kirstygallagher.com** or join her Instagram community **@kirsty_gallagher_**.

Photograph © Alice Surridge